GLUTEN FREE
RECIPES&PREPARATION

Publisher's Note: Raw or semi-cooked eggs should not be consumed by babies, toddlers, pregnant or breastfeeding women, the elderly or those suffering from a chronic illness.

The information in this book should not be treated as a substitute for professional medical advice. Neither the author nor the publisher can be held responsible for any claim or damage arising out of the use, or misuse, of the information and suggestions made in this book.

Angela Litzinger is an expert in gluten- and dairy-free recipe development and living. When not puttering around the kitchen, hanging out with her husband and three kids (or the flock of sassy chickens in the back yard), she teaches food preservation and allergen-free cooking classes, contributes articles and recipes to numerous publications, and speaks to local and national organizations about the gluten-free diet and other important allergy issues. Angela documents her family's allergen-free journey on angelaskitchen.com.

Publisher & Creative Director: Nick Wells
Senior Project Editor: Catherine Taylor
Copy Editor: Kathy Steer
Art Director: Mike Spender
Layout Design: Jane Ashley
Digital Design & Production: Chris Herbert
Proofreader: Dawn Laker

Special thanks to Laura Bulbeck, Gillian Whitaker, Carly Laird and Josh Vitchkoski

FLAME TREE PUBLISHING
6 Melbray Mews, Fulham,
London SW6 3NS, United Kingdom
www.flametreepublishing.com

This edition published 2017

Copyright © 2017 Flame Tree Publishing Ltd

17 19 21 20 18
1 3 5 7 9 10 8 6 4 2

ISBN: 978-1-78664-479-4

Images: © **StockFood** and the following: 4 Gräfe & Unzer Verlag/Schütz, Anke; 35r Hebra; 37b Lowe, Cath; 47tl Gross, Petr; 71 Gräfe & Unzer Verlag/ Zanin, Melanie; 72, 213 Gräfe & Unzer Verlag/Rynio, Jörn; 91 The Picture Pantry; 92 & back cover br Wischnewski, Jan; 96 Studer, Veronika; 101 Lehmann, Herbert; 103 Strokin, Yelena; 105 Newedel, Karl; 107 Laniak, Malgorzata; 111 Hippel, Regina; 115 Bourboulis, Spyros; 118 Janssen, Valerie; 121 Evans, Douglas; 129 Waring, Michael; 130 PhotoCuisine/Studio; 147 PhotoCuisine/Presse Citron-Barret; 169 Eising Studio - Food Photo & Video; 191 Brauner, Michael; 192 Paul, Michael; 195 Richard Jung Photography. Courtesy **Shutterstock.com** and the following: 1 & 108 Iryna Melnyk; 3, 161 pearl7; 6l, 143, 157 sarsmis; 6r Katarzyna Wojtasik; 7l AndrijaP; 7r, 136, 167 Nataliya Arzamasova; 9t, 53bl, 87 Elena Veselova; 9b Stepanek Photography; 13tl aabeele; 13b Jiri Hera; 13tr suchalinee; 14br, 47b, 49 Brent Hofacker; 14tr enchanted_fairy; 14bl ZEF; 14tl zkruger; 17b Katarzyna Hurova; 17t Sarah Noda; 19t Gita Kulinitch Studio; 19bl images72; 19br Zoroyan; 20b, 197 HandmadePictures; 20t HuanPhoto; 23br Claudio Rampinini; 23bl Olaf Speier; 23tl safakcakir; 23tr Vorontsova Anasasiia; 24 S_Photo; 27t Irina Bg; 27br spreewald.picture.de; 27bl, 35l Subbotina Anna; 28r, 57b Iakov Filimonov; 28l Lightspring; 29l Lolostock; 29r Miriam Doerr Martin Frommherz; 30, 33b g-stockstudio; 33t, 57tr Syda Productions; 34 Monkey Business Images; 37t Rostislav_Sedlacek; 38tr Peangdao; 38tl stockcreations; 38b Yulia Grigoryeva; 41t, 47tr baibaz; 41br Daxiao Productions; 41bl Lecic; 42 marekuliasz; 44b Dimitar Sotirov; 44t Pazargic Liviu; 48r JoeyPhoto; 48l Slavica Stajic; 50 pio3; 53t, 209 5 second Studio; 53br Andrey_Popov; 54t Jack Frog; 54b Virginia Garcia; 57tl jakkapan; 59bl, 63br goodmoments; 59t Matej Kastelic; 59br Pone; 60br ILEISH ANNA; 60t iravgustin; 60bl Israel Patterson; 63t Africa Studio; 63bl Venus Angel; 64l Dream79; 64r Kitch Bain; 65l Margoe Edwards; 65r tacar; 66b fototip; 66t StrelaStudio; 75 Michael Krantz; 77 GreenArt Photography; 83 photosimysia; 84 Kiian Oksana; 89 zarzamora; 113 Stephanie Jud; 123 AS Food studio; 124 AngieYeoh; 127, 149, 201 & front cover, 221 Anna Shepulova; 135 & 224 Iryna_Kolesova; 139 & back cover bl Maria Shumova; 140, 151 SEAGULL_L; 144 Foxys Forest Manufacture; 152 & back cover tr Robyn Mackenzie; 159 Elena Shashkina; 162 Liliya Kandrashevich; 164 Ilizia; 171 Viktory Panchenko; 172 Anna Kurzaeva; 177 vkuslandia; 178, 185 Losangela; 181 Adam, Frank; 187 Elena Mayne; 203 Magdalena Paluchowska; 205 & back cover tl Anna Hoychuk; 210 Oliver kite; 214 Christopher Elwell; 217 Michelle Lee Photography; and small watercolour illustrations throughout: Nadezhda Molkentin, Le Panda and Paket.

GLUTEN FREE
RECIPES&PREPARATION

Angela Litzinger

FLAME TREE
PUBLISHING

CONTENTS

Introduction — 6

What You Need to Know — 10

Staples — 68

Breakfast & Brunch — 80

Breads & Pastries — 94

Quiches, Tarts & Pizzas — 116

Light Meals & Sides — 132

Main Meals — 154

Dinner Party Dishes — 174

Sauces & Stuffings — 188

Cakes, Treats & Desserts — 198

Index — 222

INTRODUCTION

This book is the culmination of a personal journey that included years of trials, disappointments, research and joy. It is geared towards a specific and ever-increasing population, the gluten-intolerant, and it is the result of a very personal story.

When my oldest daughter was one year old, my husband and I began to notice that she was very short, thin and had many developmental delays. Shortly after her third birthday, after two years of medical testing, we were told that our daughter had coeliac (celiac) disease, a destruction of the villi in the small intestine caused by an intolerance to gluten.

As soon as we found out, we removed gluten from her diet completely and the results were amazing! Our daughter grew over 7.5 cm/3 inches in three months.

Her hair, always very thin and wispy, started to thicken and grow. She slept through the night for the first time in her life as her apnea and snoring stopped. Her language and social skills improved dramatically as she healed and started getting the nutrients she needed.

After extra therapies to help where she needed support, she has now grown from a thin, sick little girl to a strong, healthy young woman starting university studying mechanical engineering.

Coeliac turned out to be something that ran in our family. After my daughter was diagnosed with coeliac disease, several other family members, including myself, were also diagnosed.

My daughter always said she didn't miss gluten-containing foods, and as she gets very ill from the smallest accidental trace, nothing made her ever want to try to 'cheat' and eat anything that contained gluten again.

However, I couldn't help but notice the wistful looks she gave certain snacks, or her asking if there were a 'safe' version of a special treat someone had brought to school.

I missed making family favourites and wanted to keep baking my grandmother's recipes for special occasions, so I started to experiment. I began to develop a repertoire of dishes our whole family could enjoy together, but without the risk of gluten ingredients.

Later, when teaching gluten- and dairy-free cooking classes, I often asked my students what recipes they would be interested in learning. The answer was always a resounding 'EVERYTHING... how to make desserts, dinners, snacks, special-occasion dishes and breakfast items. Oh, and we want them to taste great!'

I hope you will enjoy reading and using this book as much as I enjoyed creating it.

WHAT YOU NEED
TO KNOW

WHAT IS GLUTEN?

Gluten, proteins found in wheat, barley, spelt, rye and many other grains, is a common ingredient in many recipes and food products. Gluten provides elasticity to wheat-based dough when kneaded or mixed, allowing the batter to rise by trapping the gas that is released when yeast ferments or when baking powder is activated. After baking, it helps the mixture hold together and keep its shape without crumbling or collapsing. Gluten helps foods maintain their shape and can be found in many types of foods, even in ones that would not be expected to contain gluten. It is important to read labels to catch what items contain gluten as you shop.

Gluten and gluten-containing ingredients seem to be everywhere: breads, pasta, cake, pizza… Fortunately, there is hope. These grains can easily be replaced using alternative ingredients to create delicious meals and dishes that are as good as you remember, but using safe ingredients to keep your body feeling well.

WHAT CONTAINS GLUTEN?

There are many food items that may contain gluten. Always read the label of any food you buy.

Clockwise from top left: Wheat, barley and wheat pasta

Gluten Containing Grains & Products to Avoid:

Barley

Barley malt/extract

Bran (verify source)

Brewer's yeast

Bulgur wheat

Couscous

Durum

Einkorn

Emmer

Farina

Farro

Kamut

Malt in various forms (malted milk,
   malt extract, malt syrup, malt vinegar)

Matzo flour/meal

Orzo

Panko

Rye

Seitan

Semolina

Spelt

Triticale

Udon (verify source)

Vital wheat gluten

Wheat

Wheat berries

Wheat bran

Wheat germ

What About Oats?

Many studies indicate that the protein found in oats is not harmful to most people with coeliac (celiac) disease. However, oats may be contaminated with wheat during harvest, milling and processing, so only certified gluten-free oats should be used. Due to several factors, including intolerance or the development of immune response to oat protein, similar to that which occurs due to eating gluten, people with coeliac disease should consult with their doctor or dietician before adding certified gluten-free oats to their diet.

Common Foods That Contain Gluten

BAKED GOODS, BREADS & PASTRIES

Cakes, croutons, stuffings and dressings, cookies, brownies, muffins, pitta bread, pie crusts, croissants, Danish pastries *et al.*, naan, rolls, bagels, flatbreads, cornbread, potato bread, flour tortillas.

Clockwise from top left: Seitan mock abalone, malted chocolate drink, wheat berries, oats

BEER, LAGERS, ALE, MALT BEVERAGES, MALT VINEGARS & BREWER'S YEAST

Look for products specifically made and designated as gluten-free. Since brewer's yeast is a by-product of beer, it is not generally gluten-free

BREADING & COATING MIXES

Beer batter, breadcrumbs, panko breadcrumbs.

BREAKFAST FOODS, CEREAL & GRANOLA

Waffles, pancakes, crepes, French toast, muffins, doughnuts, biscuits and cookies, energy bars. Cornflakes and rice puffs often contain malt extract/flavouring; granola and muesli are often made with regular oats, not gluten-free oats.

CRACKERS, CRISPS & CHIPS

Pretzels, soda crackers, Graham crackers and some crisp (chip) seasonings may contain malt vinegar or wheat.

FRIED FOODS

Be careful of cross-contamination from the oil if other items, with gluten-containing batter or coating, were fried in the fryer and the oil.

PASTAS & NOODLES

Spaghetti, ravioli, chow mein noodles, ramen, dumplings, udon noodles, couscous, soba noodles (unless made with 100% buckwheat flour and certified as gluten-free), egg noodles and gnocchi.

SAUCES & GRAVIES

Sauces that use wheat flour as a thickener, soy sauce (look for tamari or a gluten-free soy sauce), cream sauces made with a roux.

AND...

Anything else that uses 'wheat flour' as an ingredient.

Items That MAY Contain Gluten

Reading the label or check with the manufacturer or kitchen staff for these items:

LIP BALM, LIPSTICK & LIP GLOSS

These should be checked as they are unintentionally ingested while worn.

HERBAL, NUTRITIONAL & VITAMIN SUPPLEMENTS & MEDICATIONS

These may use gluten as a binder or gluten-containing flour as a filler.

PLAY-DOUGH & PLAY-CLAY

Children may touch their mouth or even eat wheat-based play-dough while playing with it, as well as getting it under fingernails. Make homemade versions with gluten-free flour.

STAMPS, ENVELOPES OR STICKERS

It is unlikely in the UK and the US, but the adhesive in these reportedly may contain wheat-based starch. To avoid licking them, use a small dish of water and your finger or a sponge.

BROWN RICE SYRUP

Check that it is not made with barley enzymes.

SWEETS (CANDY) & CHOCOLATE BARS

These could contain wafer, or be cross-contaminated on the production line.

CHEESECAKE FILLING

Some recipes include wheat flour.

MEAT SUBSTITUTES

Some (such as mock duck, vegetarian burgers/sausages, imitation bacon and seafood) are made with seitan, which is seasoned and prepared wheat gluten. Note that tofu is gluten-free, but be cautious of soy-sauce marinades and cross contact when eating out, especially when the tofu is fried.

COMMUNION WAFERS

Many contain a small amount of gluten.

EGGS SERVED AT RESTAURANTS

Some restaurants put pancake batter in their scrambled eggs and omelettes and cook them where pancakes are also cooked.

MULTIGRAIN TORTILLA CHIPS OR TORTILLAS

These are not entirely corn-based and may contain a wheat-based ingredient.

SOY SAUCE, SALAD DRESSINGS, MARINADES, SELF-BASTING POULTRY & PRE-SEASONED MEATS

Soy sauce often contains wheat, though tamari made without wheat is gluten-free. Dressings may contain malt vinegar, soy sauce or flour; seasonings may contain gluten.

CREAM-BASED SOUPS

These soups may have flour as a thickener. Many soups also contain barley.

STARCH OR DEXTRIN

On a meat product, this could be from any grain, including wheat.

WHEAT-FREE PRODUCTS

These are not necessarily gluten-free as they may still contain barley-based ingredients, such as spelt, rye or other ingredients, which are not gluten-free.

HOW DO YOU KNOW IF AN ITEM IS SAFE TO EAT?

Some food items are very obviously gluten-free (example: fresh fruits and vegetables, fresh cuts of meat); however, most processed food items must be questioned. Unfortunately, just reading a label cannot always tell you, as gluten can be hidden in ingredients such as modified food starch and natural flavourings. Calls to manufacturers as well as an updated gluten-free product listing (published by different support groups) are great resources.

Left: Fresh fruits, vegetables and meat are naturally gluten free

CONTAMINATION

When preparing gluten-free foods, these must not come into contact with food containing gluten. Contamination can occur if foods are prepared on common surfaces, or with utensils that are not thoroughly cleaned after preparing gluten-containing foods.

Using a common toaster for gluten-free bread and regular bread is a major source of contamination. Flour sifters should also not be shared. And as stated, deep-fried foods cooked in oil shared with breaded products should not be consumed.

Spreadable condiments in containers shared by others may also cause contamination. When a knife is dipped into a condiment for a second time, the condiment becomes contaminated with crumbs (example: mayonnaise, jam, peanut butter, margarine).

Pizzerias that offer gluten-free crusts do not always control cross-contamination with their wheat-based pizzas. Be sure to talk to the manager or chef to find out what, if any, precautions were taken. Wheat flour can stay airborne for many hours at home or in a bakery and contaminate exposed surfaces of any uncovered gluten-free products.

IF YOU AREN'T SURE ABOUT A PRODUCT, GO WITHOUT!

If you are not able to verify that ingredients for a food item are gluten-free or there is no ingredient list available, don't eat it. Adopting a strict gluten-free diet is the only known treatment for those with gluten-related disorders.

It may feel that there is so much you can't eat now, *but* read on. You'll discover there is so much more that you *can* eat. It is time to explore new cuisines and ingredients! There are so many delicious foods that are naturally gluten-free and wonderful recipes to help bring your gluten-filled family favourites back to the table with a new gluten-free makeover.

Top: Sifters and spreadable condiments should not be shared
Bottom: Gluten-free pasta and breads

WHY GLUTEN-FREE?

The last decade or so has seen a surge of interest in coeliac disease and the gluten-free diet. One boost came in 2002 from a five-year study of more than 13,000 people led by Alessio Fasano, M.D. from the University of Maryland's Center for Celiac Research. Before the study, it was assumed that coeliac disease was very rare in the United States. However, Dr Fasano's study showed the rate was more consistent with the higher numbers that were being diagnosed in other areas of the world. Coeliac disease was found in one out of every 68 adults with any coeliac-related symptoms and in one of every 22 people who had first-degree relatives with the disorder.

More interest came when the research of Joseph Murray of the Mayo Clinic was published in the July 2009 issue of *Gastroenterology*. The study was based on blood samples taken from more than 9,000 Air Force recruits between 1948 and 1954. The 50-year-old blood was tested for antibodies generated by coeliac disease. They found that 0.2 per cent of the samples had them. They then drew blood from men who were the same age as the recruits had been when their blood was drawn and from older men who were born around the same time as the recruits. When they checked these new samples, 0.9 per cent of the young men and 0.8 per cent of the older men had the antibodies for coeliac disease, suggesting that it may be 4–4½ times more common today as it was in the 1950s.

The conclusion was not just that coeliac disease may be being diagnosed more, but that something in the environment had dramatically increased the rate of coeliac disease occurring. Currently experts don't know what has changed. Some think our modern environment is so excessively sanitized that our immune systems don't get a chance to develop properly during childhood. Others suspect that the modern versions of wheat, or the constant use of gluten in the modern diet is to blame.

Whatever the reason for the increase in coeliac disease, each of you reading this right now has a unique story about why you are eating a gluten-free diet, but generally most will fall into one of the following categories:

COELIAC DISEASE

About 1 in 133 people (about 1 per cent of the population) have coeliac disease, an inherited autoimmune disease that causes damage to the small intestine when gluten

is ingested. Coeliac disease is now implicated in a huge list of symptoms beyond digestive problems, including arthritis, anaemia, infertility, a rash on the elbows and knees often mistaken for psoriasis, improper formation of tooth enamel and osteoporosis. To complicate matters further, some people with coeliac disease are asymptomatic. Doctors need to be savvy about risk factors to spot the red flags in a patient's medical history and recommend the proper tests. First, an initial blood test to detect the antibodies created when a person with coeliac disease consumes gluten and then a biopsy of the small intestine to confirm damage to intestinal villi. Anyone with a relative who has coeliac disease should be tested as well as people with other autoimmune diseases like Type 1 diabetes or thyroid disease.

What is Coeliac Disease?

Coeliac disease is an autoimmune disorder that damages or destroys the lining of the intestines in reaction to gluten, which is the protein found in wheat, barley/malt, rye, oats and all their by-products. This also includes durum, semolina, kamut and spelt.

What Are the Effects?

When a person with coeliac disease digests food containing gluten, the body mounts an immune response that attacks the small intestine. These attacks lead to damage on the villi, small finger-like projections that line the small intestine, that promote nutrient absorption. The villi produce enzymes and allow nutrients from digested food to pass into the body. If the villi are damaged and flat, the body will not be able to absorb vital nutrients such as vitamins, minerals, proteins, fats and carbohydrates.

Common Symptoms of Coeliac Disease

As there are over 200 symptoms associated with coeliac disease, it can make diagnosis difficult. A few of the symptoms may include:

- Slower or poor growth
- Irritability
- Weight loss or slow weight gain
- Bloating and cramps
- Diarrhoea
- Anaemia
- Tiredness or fatigue
- Early onset osteoporosis
- Infertility and miscarriage
- Lactose intolerance
- Vitamin and mineral deficiencies

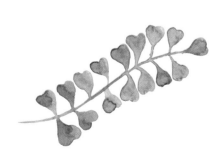

What About Dermatitis Herpetiformis?

Dermatitis Herpetiformis (DH) is a skin condition associated with coeliac disease. If you have DH, then you automatically have coeliac disease, although with less gut involvement. DH presents with itchy blisters on elbows, knees, buttocks, trunk, sacrum, face and neck that occur when gluten is ingested. The lesions are generally symmetrical in distribution. When a patient has DH, there are generally fewer intestinal symptoms and malabsorption. The majority of people with DH have intestinal damage, although 90 per cent have no intestinal symptoms.

How Common is Coeliac Disease?

Worldwide, coeliac disease is thought to occur in approximately one in 133 people. It is most common in people of European descent, and affects females about three times more often than males.

Certain populations have an increased risk of coeliac disease. For example, if someone in the family is diagnosed as coeliac, there is a high chance (95 per cent) that they carry the DQ8 and/or the DQ2 genes, which means up to 1 in 22 first-degree relatives of the person diagnosed may have coeliac disease as well. Increased risk factors can be Type 1 diabetes (1 in 23), autoimmune liver disease (1 in 12), irritable bowel syndrome (1 in 23) osteoporosis (1 in 39), Down's Syndrome (1 in 11), anaemia (1 in 24), arthritis (1 in 33), asthma (1 in 35), and Sjögren's syndrome (1 in 49) to name a few. Other autoimmune disorders associated with coeliac are the thyroid diseases, Graves and Hashimoto's thyroiditis, Addison's disease, Crohn's disease, lupus, rheumatoid arthritis, psoriasis and multiple sclerosis.

What Happens if a Coeliac Ingests Gluten – What is the Reaction Like?

A reaction will vary depending on how sensitive the individual person is and according to how much gluten was ingested. A visible reaction will usually occur within four hours of ingesting the gluten and can include stomach cramping, nausea, vomiting, headache, fatigue, irritability and diarrhoea. These symptoms can last anywhere from a few hours to several days. Some people have later-onset reactions that can include joint swelling and pain, and constipation or loose stools that can last for 2–3 weeks.

What is the Treatment for Coeliac Disease?

The treatment for coeliac disease is quite simple: a strict, lifelong diet that excludes gluten. Although simple, care must be taken as gluten can be hidden in ingredient labelling. If the diet is not followed, besides immediate reactions, there is a risk of anaemia, osteoporosis and failure to thrive, as well as a 400-per-cent-higher risk of intestinal cancer.

Anything that is ingested (for example, not just food, but beverages, medication, lipsticks, toothpaste, etc.) must be first confirmed gluten-free.

WHEAT ALLERGY

About 4 per cent of people have a doctor-diagnosed wheat allergy, according to a 2006 study. In those people, a true allergic response to wheat (which contains gluten) can include skin, respiratory and gastrointestinal symptoms.

A wheat allergy should not be confused with coeliac disease. A food allergy is an overreaction of the immune system to a specific food – usually a protein in that food. When the food is ingested, the protein triggers an allergic reaction that may include a range of symptoms from mild, such as rashes, hives or a stuffy nose, to severe, such as trouble breathing, wheezing and anaphylactic shock. A food allergy can be potentially fatal.

People who are allergic to wheat often may tolerate other grains. However, about 20 per cent of people with a wheat allergy are also allergic to other grains. Be sure to ask your doctor whether foods containing barley, rye or oats are safe for you to eat.

NON-COELIAC GLUTEN SENSITIVITY

A larger group of people is estimated to have what's called non-coeliac gluten sensitivity (NCGS), which may also produce similar symptoms to coeliac disease or wheat allergy, but when both have been ruled out, and the patient still improves on a gluten-free diet. According to the National Foundation for Celiac Awareness, as many as 18 million Americans have some non-coeliac sensitivity to gluten. A lot about this condition, like its pathophysiology, epidemiology and treatments, are still unclear and being researched.

OTHER REASONS TO GO GLUTEN-FREE

There are a variety of reasons others may decide to follow a gluten-free diet: to combat inflammation, as a treatment for autism, weight loss or for general health support. Whatever reason you have for following a gluten-free diet, be sure to start with the guidance of a nutritionist or doctor to make sure all the nutrients needed are making their way into your diet. Stick with a wide variety of whole foods, gluten-free grains, fats and protein sources to best fill in any missing pieces nutritionally.

KEY GLUTEN-FREE FOODS

Going gluten-free can seem like a challenge at first, but a well-stocked store cupboard can make the transition a whole lot easier. By keeping a few staples on hand at all times, you can create lots of delicious meals that satisfy your dietary needs and your taste buds. It can be very tempting to eat something that's filled with gluten just because it's easy or more convenient, but having a stocked store cupboard will make eating gluten-free just as easy.

GLUTEN-FREE STAPLES TO HAVE IN THE KITCHEN

Protein Sources

Eggs, wild fish (salmon, cod, herring, trout, sardines), shellfish and molluscs (prawns/shrimp, crab, lobster, mussels, clams, oysters), meats (pork, beef, lamb, liver, chicken, turkey, duck), wild game, legumes and lentils, nuts (almonds, cashews, peanuts, pecans, walnuts, hazelnuts) and seeds (flaxseed, sunflower seeds, pumpkin seeds, sesame seeds, chia seeds).

Vegetables

Leafy greens and lettuces, collard greens, (bell) peppers, cucumbers, tomatoes, courgettes (zucchini), squashes, pumpkins, aubergines (eggplants), spinach, broccoli, kale, chard, cabbage, carrots, onions, mushrooms, cauliflower, Brussels sprouts, sauerkraut, artichokes, alfalfa sprouts, green beans, celery, pak choi, radishes, watercress, turnips, asparagus, garlic, leeks, fennel, shallots, potatoes, sweet potatoes, spring onions (scallions), ginger.

Fruits

Strawberries, blueberries, grapes, cranberries, figs, dates, nectarines, blackberries, apples, apricots, cherries, bananas, plums, peaches, lemons, mangoes, melons, limes, oranges and clementines.

Gluten-free Whole Grains

Brown rice, quinoa, sorghum, wild rice, amaranth, teff, buckwheat, millet, gluten-free certified oats.

Healthy Fats

Extra virgin olive oil, coconut oil, avocado oil, grass-fed butter, ghee, flaxseed oil and sesame oil. It can also include avocados, olives, coconuts and nut and seed butters.

Herbs, Seasonings & Condiments

All single herbs and spices should be gluten-free. This includes salt, black pepper, allspice, nutmeg, onion powder, cinnamon, ground ginger, cloves, garlic powder, basil, chili powder, caraway seeds, etc. Just be sure to check labels to make sure you are buying herbs, spices and seasonings that are gluten-free and uncontaminated.

Depending on what country you live in or brand you buy, ketchup, mustard, chutney, BBQ sauce, mayonnaise, tartar sauce, taco sauce and Worcestershire sauce may not contain gluten. Horseradish, tapenade and salsa are generally free from gluten. A lot of soy sauces contain gluten, so look for one that is gluten-free or look for wheat-and-gluten-free tamari sauce. Vinegars are gluten-free, except for malt vinegar.

BAKING INGREDIENTS

Raising Agents, Sweeteners and Flavourings

Baking powder (double check if gluten-free), bicarbonate of soda (baking soda), fast-action dried yeast (baking or active dry yeast), cream of tartar, sugar, brown sugar, honey, molasses, maple syrup, icing (confectioners') sugar, pure gluten-free vanilla and almond extracts, cocoa, chocolate chips (be sure they are gluten-free).

Gluten-free Flours & Binders

RICE FLOUR

Milled from unpolished brown rice, brown rice flour has a higher nutrient value than white rice flour. Since it contains bran, it has a shorter shelf life and should be refrigerated. White rice flour is ground from white rice. With brown and white rice flour, it is best to combine them with several other flours to avoid the grainy texture.

BEAN FLOURS

Flour made from chickpeas, beans, or in combination with broad (fava) beans. Combine with sorghum to cut the taste of the beans.

CORNMEAL

Ground from dried corn, this can be made from yellow, white or blue corn.

BUCKWHEAT FLOUR

From the seed of a plant related to rhubarb, this is high in fibre, iron and B vitamins.

SORGHUM FLOUR

Made from the grain of a flowering plant in the grass family *Poaceae*, this has a neutral taste, and is slightly sweet. Its light colour makes it easily adaptable to a variety of dishes.

Top: Bicarbonate of soda (baking soda). Bottom: Maize and cornmeal

QUINOA FLOUR

A staple food of the Incas, quinoa is a complete protein containing all 8 amino acids as well as a fair amount of calcium and iron, and is high in some B vitamins and folic acid.

AMARANTH FLOUR

A whole grain dating from the time of the Aztecs, this is high in protein and contains more calcium, folic acid and Vitamins A, C and E than most grains.

MILLET FLOUR

A small round grain, millet is a rich source of B vitamins.

OAT FLOUR

Milled from oats, oat flour is a great source of dietary fibre.

TEFF FLOUR

An ancient grain from Ethiopia, this is always manufactured as a wholegrain flour. It is a good source of protein, calcium, iron, fibre and B vitamins.

CHESTNUT, ALMOND AND OTHER NUT FLOURS

High in protein and used in small amounts in recipes, finely ground nut flours enhance the taste of many baked goods and allow for a better rise. They are a great substitute for non-fat dried milk powder in gluten-free recipes.

SWEET RICE FLOUR

Milled from 'sticky rice', this has a much higher starch content than other rice flours and has great binding properties. Used more as a starch than a flour in gluten-free baking.

POTATO FLOUR

Made from whole, peeled potatoes, potato flour attracts moisture to baked goods.

POTATO STARCH

Starch from potatoes, this is a great replacement for cornflour (cornstarch) – which is a

Clockwise from top left: Quinoa flour; various gluten-free flours (chick pea, rice, buckwheat, amaranth, almond); bread made with amaranth flour

bonus for those with a corn allergy or who are on a diet that limits grain consumption. It adds moisture to baked goods.

TAPIOCA FLOUR (STARCH)

Made from the root of the cassava plant, tapioca flour helps bind and improve the texture of baked goods. It also helps add chew and crispness to crusts.

CORNFLOUR (CORNSTARCH)

Made from the endosperm of corn, this contributes a tender texture and browner crust.

ARROWROOT

Made from the roots of the arrowroot plant, this can be used as a direct substitute for cornflour (cornstarch).

XANTHAN GUM

This acts as an emulsifier and binder, adding volume and stretch to baked goods.

Above left: Gluten-free grains and flours. Above right: Arrowroot plant

GUAR GUM

This is a white flour-like substance made from an East Indian seed used as a binder like xanthan gum. It can be used interchangeably with xanthan gum.

OTHER ITEMS TO KEEP ON HAND

- Non-dairy beverages (such as almond or coconut milk)
- Tea and coffee (unflavoured are generally gluten-free)
- Canned pumpkin
- Unsweetened apple purée (sauce)
- Dried fruit
- Pre-made pasta
- Pasta sauce and chopped tomatoes
- Corn tortillas

GOING GLUTEN-FREE

It isn't always easy to adjust to the gluten-free life, but there are simple ways to make the transition much easier.

BE PATIENT

It is easy to be overwhelmed by change, and the challenge of eating gluten-free can feel like a big change. At first it might seem like the diet eliminates all the food you love to eat. It could take up to six months to begin to feel comfortable with the diet and confident about your food choices. Give yourself time to adjust and don't be hard on yourself for accidental exposure to gluten. It can happen as you are learning. Don't expect to have it all figured out overnight. It will get easier over time as you learn more.

It is normal to feel grief over having to give up foods you have eaten your whole life. I find this is especially true for people during the holiday seasons. I chose to combat this by taking just one recipe every year or two from my grandmother and converting it to be gluten-free. I did this instead of working on the whole meal. Having just one recipe to focus on converting helped me ensure success in the long run and, over time, all of the meal is now made gluten-free.

STAY POSITIVE

Concentrate on what you can eat, not on what you can't eat. Remember that most of the nutritious foods you are supposed to eat to stay healthy are naturally gluten-free. This includes plain meat, fish, poultry, beans, eggs, vegetables, fruits, rice, nuts, herbs, spices and legumes. When you would like a treat, there are now plenty of options to choose from in the market place when you get a craving for something you haven't learned to make from scratch. Try not to rely on pre-made processed foods for all your meals (you're trying to regain your health, right?), but for the occasional treat, or if you have a particularly busy day, it is nice to know the options are out there.

CHOOSE WHOLE FOODS

Remember that just because something is labelled gluten-free does not mean it is good for you. When first going gluten-free, all the prepared products can be very tempting. However, a doughnut is still a doughnut whether it is gluten-free or not. Concentrate at first on eating plain, healthy foods to regain your health. When you are feeling better and your confidence in your gluten-free choices is higher, then take the time to experiment more in the kitchen with more ambitious recipes. If a cooking experiment goes awry? Take the time to laugh, enjoy the process and try again.

MEET OTHERS

Get in touch with others who are going through the same thing as you are. Check for local support groups or check online for others who are living gluten-free. Others have been where you are right now, trying to figure it out and can help guide you through what worked for them, recommend favourite gluten-free friendly restaurants and share recipes. I can't tell you how amazing it was the first time I was able to bring my daughter to a play date and we didn't have to pack a snack or worry about gluten-containing play-dough because that family ate gluten-free as well and got what we were going through.

GET READY TO RESEARCH & LEARN NEW THINGS

As with all new ventures, gather all the information you can about the gluten-free diet. Stick with reputable sources for your information to weed out conflicting advice from unverified sources. Work with a nutritionist, dietitian or doctor specializing in coeliac or gluten-free diets to help start you on the right path with solid information.

BECOME A LABEL READER & SHOP AROUND

While your local market may have all the things you need, check out other grocers, health food stores, shops, even online to see what they have in stock. Different markets carry different things and the price point can vary greatly. You would be amazed at the different products out there.

That being said, be sure to read labels and check it is safe for eating on the gluten-free diet. Remember, wheat-free doesn't mean it is also gluten-free! Companies can change the formula of their products, so it pays to read the label on products every time you buy them.

Don't try to figure out all the products at once. As you start eating gluten-free, try to mainly shop the perimeter of the market, choosing whole fruits, vegetables and proteins. Pick out only one or two products to read or to research. If you have a smartphone, there are several apps that are updated continuously that allow you to check the gluten-free status on a number of products and medications.

LOOK FOR GLUTEN-FREE-CERTIFIED PRODUCTS

When shopping, seeing a seal of certification from one of the groups that certifies gluten-free foods can give you increased confidence that it is a safe product. These seals guarantee not only that the product's ingredients are gluten-free, but ensure that there was not cross-contamination during the manufacturing process.

PLAN AHEAD

Making a menu plan helps when shopping. Not only can it keep your budget under control, but you won't be tempted to buy things not on the list that contain gluten when you know what it is you will be making that week. Freeze leftovers as individual meals for days you are too busy to cook. Keep a stock of gluten-free snacks and other food on hand that are portable for those times when you know you will be away for several hours and unsure of where to eat safely. I like to keep a stash of gluten-free cupcakes in my freezer for impromptu birthday celebrations. Just bring your own cupcake. The gathering is about the friends, not the food, but having a cupcake you can safely eat? That's the icing on the cake!

TOOLS & EQUIPMENT

When you go gluten-free, you will inevitably spend some time in the kitchen, so it is a good idea to get a few tools to help you cook up some great meals. It can take only the smallest bit of gluten to cause problems for a gluten-intolerant person. As you get started, there are a few things to clean and a few things you may need to replace in your kitchen to avoid gluten contamination in your home. Don't worry, you don't have to toss everything out, but remember if you live with others who are still eating gluten, you will have to be extra careful.

A WORD ABOUT CROSS-CONTAMINATION

Be sure to explain what is happening to your family and friends. A knife which has spread mayo on gluten bread and then been put back into the jar has contaminated the whole container with those gluten-y crumbs. I suggest a separate jar that is labelled 'Gluten-free'. I know a few people who have a separate cabinet that is entirely dedicated to their gluten-free items. In our house, which is all gluten- and dairy-free, we have the opposite situation. We have a cupboard area for any gluten-containing items that make it into our house. Condiments in the refrigerator that may contain gluten and dairy are very clearly marked and kept in a contained area.

A HEAVY-DUTY STAND MIXER

Many of the gluten-free batters and doughs are much heavier and stickier than their gluten-filled counterparts, so a heavy-duty stand mixer is a must for every gluten-free kitchen. You will definitely want to invest in a good stand mixer if you are planning to experiment with yeasted bread recipes, many of which require mixing on high for at least 3 minutes to help develop the elasticity needed for the recipe to be successful. Try not to skimp on your mixer and get the one with the sturdiest motor that you can afford.

TOASTERS

Some people who follow a gluten-free diet use specially designed toaster bags to toast their gluten-free bread in a gluten-designated toaster. However, I recommend buying an extra toaster and designating it for gluten-free use *only*, since toasters cannot be cleaned. We have two toasters in our house in completely separate areas – one for gluten-filled breads and one for gluten-free breads, both clearly labelled. Remember toasters toss crumbs about when the toast pops, so keep the gluten toaster in an area where it won't contaminate your gluten-free food or where the crumbs can be tracked all over the kitchen.

CAN OPENER

Be sure to check the blades of the can opener for bits of caked-on food. Scrub it down or get a new one and label it for gluten-free only.

PLASTIC BOWLS

Plastic can be porous and scratches in plastic can harbour hidden gluten. Check all plastic bowls and replace any that are scratched.

COOKING POTS & BAKING SHEETS

Unfortunately, these can be a major source of contamination. With pots and pans, you will need to carefully take stock. The big tip for deciding if you need to replace any of your cookware: if it is made of a porous material – sorry, it will have to be replaced.

NONSTICK PANS

Nonstick that is scratched will definitely have to be replaced. There is not an effective way to clean the crevices to make sure it is not contaminated with gluten. The surfaces of nonstick pans are also very porous, so they will be contaminated by gluten-containing foods that have been cooked in it in the past.

CAST-IRON PANS

Because cast-iron pans build up a layer of 'seasoning' that makes it nonstick and keeps the pan from rusting, this layer has gluten trapped all the way through it. Either replace them or have them resurfaced and re-season.

STAINLESS-STEEL PANS

Inspect stainless-steel pans carefully for a layer of burnt oil build-up. Stainless steel can be scoured until it is shiny and new-looking.

STONEWARE

These porous pans have that 'seasoning' you have worked so hard to develop to create a nonstick surface. Unfortunately, this will cross-contaminate your food with gluten trapped in the seasoning. I found stoneware expensive to replace, so a friend who is not-gluten intolerant and I traded pans. She was thrilled to get an already seasoned stoneware pan and I got a new un-used pan all ready to go.

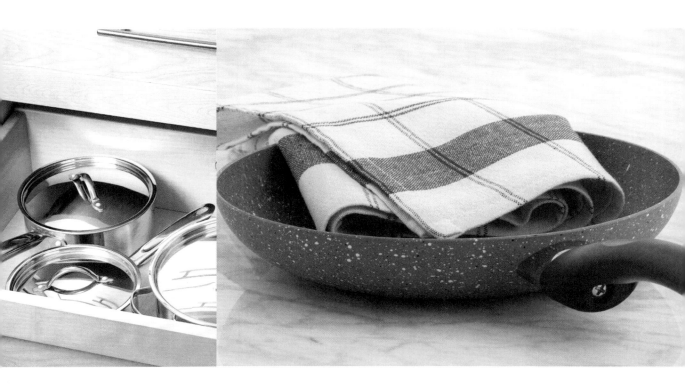

UTENSILS, CHOPPING BOARDS & OTHER KITCHEN TOOLS

If you still have gluten being cooked in your home, old chopping (cutting) boards, wooden or nonstick utensils and pans can be kept separate from the 'gluten-free' pans and utensils. Designate separate storage cupboards for them.

Flour Sifters, Colanders & Sieves

It is impossible to clean the tiny particles of flour or pasta residue out of the little holes in these tools effectively. Replace them, or get a second set designated for gluten-free use.

Wooden Chopping Boards, Wooden Spoons, Wooden Rolling Pins

Wood is porous, so anything that has been used to prepare gluten-containing food cannot be used to fix gluten-free food. Grandma's antique rolling pin can stay if you clean it carefully and hang it on a display rack.

Replace All Chopping Boards

Gluten cannot be cleaned effectively from the deep scratches and cuts on the boards.

Some Final Tips

You don't need to break the bank replacing all of your cooking equipment right away. Replace only what you really need to, or just avoid using it for now. For baking pans, don't forget you can use baking parchment or foil to line them, so don't purchase new ones immediately. Really, all you need is an uncontaminated frying pan with a lid, a saucepan with a lid and a larger stock/pasta/chili/soup pot with a lid – a steamer insert is nice for this last one, as well. Decide what you need now in order to make your gluten-free food, then, as you need different things and try new recipes, replace them as you can and as you need them.

STAPLES

BEAN FLOUR BLEND

Garfava is a blend of chickpea (garbanzo) and broad (fava) beans. If you can't find it, then replace it with chickpea flour. You can easily double or triple this recipe.

Makes about 1.2 kg / 2³⁄₄ lb / 9 cups

385 g/13½ oz/3 cups cornflour (cornstarch) or arrowroot flour
330 g/11¾ oz/3 cups tapioca flour (tapioca starch)
240 g/8½ oz/2 cups garfava bean flour
125 g/4 oz/1 cup sorghum flour

Whisk all the ingredients together well. Store in an airtight container for up to 6 months.

NOTE – USING XANTHAN OR GUAR GUM IN FLOURS

To help with the texture of gluten-free baked goods, add xanthan or guar gum to the gluten-free flour in your recipe. It will help keep things from crumbling and give bounce and stretch. Use the following proportions:

Per 120 g / 4 oz / 1 cup flour add:	Xanthan gum	Guar Gum
Cookies	¼ tsp	¼–½ tsp
Cakes & Pancakes	½ tsp	¾ tsp
Muffins & Quick Breads	¾ tsp	1 tsp
Yeast Breads	1–1½ tsp	1½–2 tsp
Pizza Dough	2 tsp	1 tbsp

Right: Guar gum

RICE-SORGHUM FLOUR BLEND

You can easily double or triple this recipe.

Makes about 1.3 kg / 2³⁄₄ lb / 9 cups

500 g/1 lb 2 oz/3¾ cups brown rice flour

250 g/9 oz/2¼ cups sorghum flour

256 g/9 oz/2 cups cornstarch or arrowroot powder

150 g/5 oz/¾ cup potato starch (not potato flour)

40 g/1½ oz/¼ cup potato flour (not potato starch)

Whisk all the ingredients together well. Store in an airtight container for up to 6 months.

VARIATIONS & SUBSTITUTIONS IN FLOUR BLENDS

Vary these flour recipes to work for you – just replace with the same weight you are removing:

- For structure and stability, use 30–40% by weight of higher-protein, mild-flavour flours, such as brown/white rice, amaranth, sorghum, buckwheat, chickpea, millet, oat, quinoa.

- For lighter/softer texture, use 30-40% by weight of starch-based flours, such as corn flour (cornstarch), kudzu root starch, potato starch, arrowroot, sweet potato flour, tapioca starch.

- For better mouth-feel and crispier, browner crusts, use 30% tapioca flour (starch).

- Optional add-in – for fibre, nutrition, added moisture, taste and interest, use 10–15% additional flours, such as teff, almond/other nuts, coconut, buckwheat, flax, potato (not starch), cornmeal, chickpea, mesquite, oat, quinoa, chia seed.

Left: Rice-sorghum flour with teff

BASIC GLUTEN-FREE BREAD

This is the base gluten-free, dairy-free bread I make every week for our family. For variety, add toasted nuts or sweet raisins and cinnamon.

Makes 1 loaf/ Serves 14

2 tbsp vegetable oil, plus extra for oiling

175 ml/6 fl oz/scant ¾ cup room-temperature milk or dairy-free substitute, such as rice or almond, plus up to 2 tbsp depending on bread dough texture

63 g/2¼ oz/½ cup chickpea flour

35 g/1¼ oz/ ¼ cup sorghum flour

2¼ tsp easy-blend dried dry (active baking) yeast

2 tbsp granulated sugar or sweetener of choice

1 tsp cider vinegar

2 medium (large) eggs, at room temperature

65 g/2½ oz/½ cup cornflour (cornstarch)

95 g/3¼ oz/½ cup potato starch

65 g/2½ oz/½ cup tapioca flour (starch)

1 tbsp xanthan gum

1 tsp salt

Oil a 450 g/1 lb (20 x 10 cm/8 x 4 inch) loaf pan well with oil and set aside.

Combine 175 ml/6 fl oz/scant ¾ cup milk with the flours, yeast, sugar and vinegar in a non-reactive bowl. Mix well, then cover and set aside for 2–4 hours.

Beat the eggs until frothy in a heavy-duty stand mixer. Add the oil and blend, then add the chickpea flour mixture and stir well.

Whisk the dry ingredients together in another bowl, then add them to the mixer bowl, mixing well on low speed until everything is incorporated. Check the texture of the dough. If needed, add 1 tablespoon milk at a time until the correct texture is achieved. The dough should not be too stiff and dry, or thin and soupy. It will be very thick and sticky. Beat on high speed for 3 minutes. Scoop the dough into the loaf pan and smooth the top with oiled hands. Cover with oiled plastic wrap and leave to rise in a warm place for 20–45 minutes. Do not let the dough rise past the top of the pan or it will be over-proved.

Preheat the oven to 190°C/375°F/Gas Mark 5, and bake for 50–60 minutes. If the crust is browning too much, cover the top with foil during the last half of the baking time. Cool in the pan for 5 minutes, then remove and cool completely on a wire rack.

Tip

Place ice on an old baking pan and put it in the oven on the bottom rack. Place the bread on the rack above in the centre of the oven. As it bakes, the loaf will get steam from the ice.

SHORTCRUST PASTRY

Light and flaky gluten-free pastry is simple to make. Keep some in the freezer so you can make a quick tart when fruit is in season.

Makes a generous-sized double crust

40 g/1½ oz/⅓ cup finely ground brown rice flour

40 g/1½ oz/⅓ cup sorghum flour

65 g/2½ oz/⅔ cup tapioca flour (tapioca starch)

130 g/4½ oz/⅔ cup potato starch

2 tbsp cornflour (cornstarch)

4 tsp granulated sugar

1½ tsp gluten-free baking powder

1 tbsp xanthan gum

1 tsp salt

225 g/8 oz/1 cup cold shortening or lard, cut into 2.5 cm/1 inch chunks

1 cold medium (large) egg or flaxseed equivalent (using golden flaxseed: 1 tbsp
   ground flax mixed in 2 tbsp warm water)

2 tsp apple cider vinegar

2 tbsp ice-cold water, plus 50 ml/2 fl oz/¼ cup extra ice cold water, as needed

Whisk the flours, potato starch, cornflour (cornstarch), sugar, baking powder, xanthan gum and salt together in a large bowl. Using a pastry cutter, fork or table knife, cut the cold shortening into the dry ingredients until pea-size or smaller.

Beat the egg with the vinegar and 2 tablespoons of the water. Pour the egg mixture over the flour mixture and toss together with a fork. If more water is needed so the dough holds together when squeezed, then sprinkle 1 tablespoon of the water at a time onto the dough. Using your hands, form the dough into 2 balls, then place each ball onto a sheet of plastic wrap and flatten into a disc, about 2.5–4 cm/1–1½ inches thick. Wrap well in the plastic wrap and chill for at least 1 hour.

Working with one disc at a time, unwrap and place the dough between two sheets of plastic wrap on the work surface. Roll out until you achieve the desired thickness. The dough should be about 4 cm/1½ inches larger in diameter than the pie pan.

Peel the top sheet of plastic wrap away from the dough. Slip your hand underneath the dough and base plastic wrap, then using the plastic wrap to help support the dough, gently flip the dough into the pie pan, plastic wrap side up. Remove the plastic. Trim the excess dough or crimp the edges to form a decorative border. Bake as needed for your recipe.

Tip

To freeze discs of dough, wrap them well in plastic wrap and place in a large freezer bag, removing as much air as possible and freeze. To use, allow the dough to thaw overnight in the refrigerator. When thawed, shape and bake as directed.

HOMEMADE PASTA

You can easily double or even triple this recipe. Work with the pasta in batches if you do, covering the pasta not being shaped with a clean, lightly damp tea (dish) towel.

Serves 4 as a main dish

150 g/5 oz/1 cup finely ground white rice flour, plus extra for dusting

50 g/2 oz/⅓ cup potato starch, plus extra for dusting

1 tbsp cornflour (cornstarch)

2 tbsp xanthan gum

¼ tsp salt

3 large (extra large) eggs

1 tbsp olive oil

Pulse all the ingredients in a food processor. When the ingredients have come together into a rough dough, tip out onto a work surface dusted with rice flour and potato starch and knead for 4–5 minutes until the dough is very smooth.

Shape Pasta Using a Pasta Machine

Using a pasta machine, cut the ball of dough into quarters and roll out each piece of dough to slightly less than 1.5 cm/⅝ inch thick. Lightly dust the dough with potato starch and place each piece between baking parchment if needed to keep it from sticking to the pasta machine. Run the dough through the pasta machine, starting at a wide setting, then decreasing the setting width for each pass of the pasta dough until the dough is as thin as desired. If the pasta sheet starts to break or crack, it is thin enough. Cut fettuccine, spaghetti or ravioli following the machine's instructions.

Shape Pasta by Hand

To cut the dough by hand, cut the dough into 8 pieces, then cut each of those pieces in half, so they are about the size of golf balls. Roll out each piece of dough as thin as you possibly can with a rolling pin.

For long cuts of pasta, lightly dust the pasta sheet with potato starch and roll up, starting from the narrowest end. Cut resulting spiral of dough about 5 mm/¼ inch wide for fettuccine, cutting thinner for spaghetti.

For ravioli, cut the rolled-out pasta into 5 cm/2 inch square pieces. Beat 1 egg with 1 tablespoon water to make an egg wash. Spoon a small amount of desired filling in the middle of a pasta square, then brush the edges of the pasta square with the egg wash. Top with another pasta square and press down around the edge to seal the ravioli.

For lasagne, leave the pasta in long sheets that fit your baking pan.

Cook Pasta

To cook pasta, bring a large pan of salted water to the boil. Put the pasta shape of your choice into the boiling water. When the pasta rises to the surface, take a little piece and taste it. You should be able to bite into it without it falling apart. Gluten-free pasta cooks much faster than gluten-based pasta. If it is close, be sure to watch carefully so that it does not overcook and become mushy.

Cooking times will vary for the different shapes: ravioli will cook in 5–6 minutes, fettuccine in 4–5 minutes and spaghetti in 3–4 minutes depending on thickness.

Variations

Add the flavour variations to the eggs and purée until smooth before adding to pasta.

Spinach: 75 g/3 oz/½ cup thawed frozen spinach, squeezed very dry.

Beetroot (beet): One small beetroot, roasted and puréed. About 40 g/1½ oz/¼ cup.

Saffron: 4 saffron strands soaked in 2 tablespoons warm water for 30 minutes.

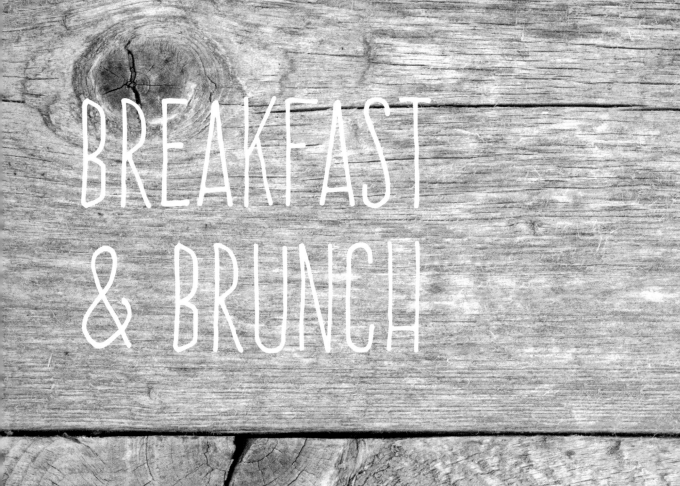

BREAKFAST & BRUNCH

RICE-FLOUR PANCAKES

Light fluffy pancakes are fantastic to serve on a lazy weekend morning. They are also great served with gluten-free sausages and fruit as a fast, fun 'breakfast for dinner' weeknight meal.

Serves 4 / makes 16–18

130 g/4½ oz/1 cup each finely ground white rice flour and brown rice flour

50 g/2 oz/¼ cup granulated sugar

4 tsp gluten-free baking powder

1¼ tsp xanthan gum

½ tsp salt

500 ml/18 fl oz/2 cups milk or milk substitute of choice

2 medium (large) eggs

2 tbsp vegetable oil, plus extra for cooking

Whisk the rice flours, sugar, baking powder, xanthan gum and salt together in a bowl. Beat in the milk until the mixture is very smooth. Add the eggs and oil, mixing until just blended. Leave to stand for 20–30 minutes.

Heat a well-oiled frying pan or griddle over a medium-high heat. Spoon 2 rounded tablespoons of the batter into the hot pan and cook until bubbles begin to form. Flip the pancake and continue cooking until golden brown on the base. Depending on the size of your pan, make 2–3 pancakes at a time. Serve immediately with toppings of your choice.

Variations

Bean Flour: For a little more protein and fibre, replace the rice flours with the Bean Flour Blend (*see* page 70). Use 3 tablespoons maple syrup to replace the sugar.

Cinnamon Oat Pancakes: Substitute 85 g/3¼ oz/1 cup gluten-free certified oats, pulsed slightly in a blender, for 130 g/4½ oz/1 cup rice flour. You can also use quinoa flakes in the same ratio, but no need to pulse them. Replace the sugar with brown sugar and add 1 teaspoon ground cinnamon to the batter.

Apple or Pear Pancakes: Add 125 g/4 oz/1 cup finely chopped peeled apple or pear, ½ teaspoon ground cinnamon and ¼ teaspoon ground nutmeg.

Bacon Pancakes: Replace the sugar with 3 tablespoons maple syrup. Add 12 rashers (slices)/¾ cup crispy cooked and crumbled bacon.

Chocolate Pancakes: Add 1–2 tablespoons desired sweetener and 1 melted square of dark (unsweetened) chocolate. Stir 125 g/4 oz/¾ cup gluten-free chocolate chips into batter, if liked.

CORN FRITTERS

For an unexpected pop of flavour, fold very finely chopped jalapeño chilies (peppers), thinly sliced spring onions (scallions) or caramelized onions into the batter with the sweetcorn.

Serves 4

350 g/12 oz/2 cups cornmeal

1 tsp gluten-free baking powder

salt and freshly ground black pepper

2 medium (large) eggs

200 ml/7 fl oz/¾ cup milk or unsweetened dairy-free substitute

50 ml/2 fl oz/¼ cup honey

50 ml/2 fl oz/¼ cup olive oil

330 g/11¾ oz/2 cups sweetcorn, fresh or frozen

vegetable oil, for cooking

Mix the cornmeal, baking powder and ¼ teaspoon salt together in a bowl. Add the eggs, milk, honey and oil and mix well. Fold in the sweetcorn.

Heat the oil in a frying pan over a medium-high heat. Scoop 2 tablespoons of the batter into the pan, flattening slightly to create a patty shape, if needed, and fry for 5–7 minutes on each side until the fritter is golden brown and cooked through. Remove, then cover with a tea (dish) towel while the rest of the fritters are cooked. Repeat until all the batter is used. Season.

CHICKPEA COURGETTE WAFFLES
with Eggs

Waffles don't need to only be made as a sweet breakfast treat. Serve this courgette (zucchini) speckled waffle with fresh basil, vine-ripened tomatoes and a poached egg for a summer brunch that is hard to beat.

Serves 4

For the chickpea courgette waffles

250 g/9 oz/2 cups chickpea flour

2 tsp salt

1½ tsp gluten-free baking powder

¼ tsp freshly ground black pepper

½ tsp xanthan gum

250 ml/8 fl oz/1 cup milk or unsweetened dairy-free substitute

2 medium (large) eggs, separated

1 courgette (zucchini), coarsely grated

3 tbsp olive oil

2 tbsp very finely chopped basil, plus extra to garnish

1 garlic clove, peeled and very finely chopped

olive or vegetable oil spray, for cooking

For the tomatoes & eggs

1 tsp cider vinegar

4 large (extra large) eggs

2–3 heirloom vine-ripened tomatoes, sliced

Preheat the oven to 110°C/225°F/Gas Mark ¼ and line a baking sheet with baking parchment. Preheat a waffle iron according to the manufacturer's instructions.

To make the waffles, combine the flour, salt, baking powder, pepper and xanthan gum in a bowl. In another bowl, whisk the milk, egg yolks, courgette (zucchini), oil, basil and garlic together. Stir the wet ingredients into the dry and mix well.

Using a freestanding mixer with a whisk attachment, beat the egg whites until fluffy, then fold them into the batter until there are no more streaks of white.

When the waffle iron reaches the desired temperature, lightly spray with oil and pour the recommended amount of batter into the iron. Cook according to the manufacturer's instructions. Transfer the cooked waffle to the prepared baking sheet and keep warm. Repeat with the remaining batter.

For the eggs, fill a frying pan two-thirds full with water, add the vinegar and bring to the boil. Reduce the heat to a simmer, break each egg into a small cup and pour gently into the pan. Cook for 3 minutes or to your liking. Carefully remove the eggs with a slotted spoon. Serve with the waffles and tomato slices and garnish with extra fresh basil.

AMARANTH & QUINOA PORRIDGE

Enjoy this porridge on chilly autumn mornings with a dollop of whipped almond butter for a breakfast that will fill you up until lunchtime. This recipe can easily be halved or doubled.

Serves 4 / makes 175 g / 6 oz / ³/₄ cup

For the whipped almond butter

125 g/4 oz/½ cup almond butter, not the 'stir-in' version

½ tsp gluten-free vanilla extract

¼ tsp ground cinnamon

3–6 tbsp almond milk

For the porridge

125 g/4 oz/⅔ cup amaranth, rinsed

125 g/4 oz/⅔ cup black, red or white quinoa, well rinsed

700 ml/24 fl oz/3 cups water

150 ml/5 fl oz/⅔ cup milk or almond milk

3 tbsp honey, maple syrup or agave syrup

To serve (optional)

whipped almond butter (see recipe)

blueberries

plain dark (semisweet) chocolate

dash ground cinnamon or cocoa powder

For the butter, cream the butter, vanilla and cinnamon in a high-power blender. Add 1 tablespoon milk at a time, whisking on high speed between additions, then scraping down the bowl until the mixture becomes light and fluffy. Set aside.

For the porridge, stir the amaranth, quinoa and water together in a saucepan. Bring to the boil, then reduce the heat and simmer, uncovered, stirring occasionally for 20 minutes until most of the water has been absorbed.

Stir in the milk and honey and simmer for 10 minutes until the grains are cooked. Leave to stand for 5 minutes. Serve with the toppings.

Store the almond butter in the refrigerator for up to a week.

GOLDEN OVERNIGHT OATS
with Chia Pudding Variation

I like to drink golden milk made with coconut milk on its own in the evening, so it was natural to use it in this overnight-oats breakfast. I love how the chai-inspired spices enhance the flavour even more!

Serves 4

175 g/6 oz/2 cups gluten-free certified old-fashioned rolled oats

2 tbsp chia seeds

1 tbsp hemp hearts

1 tbsp ground golden flaxseed

1 tsp ground turmeric

¼ tsp ground cinnamon

¼ tsp ground ginger

¼ tsp ground cardamom

dash freshly ground black pepper

500 ml/18 fl oz/2 cups milk or dairy-free alternative, such as coconut milk

2 tbsp maple syrup

½ tsp gluten-free vanilla extract

To serve

fruit of choice

honey, for drizzling (optional)

Stir all the dry ingredients together in a large bowl. Add the wet ingredients to the dry and stir to combine well. Cover and chill overnight. Stir before serving with fruit and a drizzle of honey, if liked.

To make individual servings, divide the mixture between 4 screw-top jars or bowls. Cover and chill overnight.

Variation

Replace the oats with 50 g/2 oz/⅓ cup chia seeds. After stirring everything together, leave to stand for 20 minutes, then stir to redistribute the seeds and break up any clumps. Cover and chill overnight. Stir before serving.

ALMOND CREPES

These crepes are incredibly easy to make and can be filled with different things depending on your mood, such as vanilla yogurt and berries.

Serves 4 / makes 8–10

For the crepes

100 g/3½ oz/1 cup very finely ground almond flour

50 g/2 oz/½ cup tapioca flour (tapioca starch)

4 medium (large) eggs

250 ml/8 fl oz/1 cup milk or dairy-free alternative, such as almond milk

pinch salt

2–3 tbsp coconut oil or knob (pat) butter

Optional additions

1 tbsp maple syrup

½ tsp ground cardamom

½ tsp gluten-free vanilla extract

Place all the ingredients, except the coconut oil or butter, in a blender and blend until smooth.

Heat the oil in a crepe or small frying pan and turn the pan to coat the base evenly with the oil.

Scoop 3–4 tablespoons of the batter into the pan and let it spread out. Once the crepe has started to become firm, flip it over and cook the other side until done. Remove from the pan, cover with a tea (dish) towel and repeat until all the batter is used.

Serve with the filling of your choice.

BREADS & PASTRIES

GLUTEN-FREE CROISSANTS

It is best to make this on a cool day, as, in order for the dough to bake with flakier layers, the butter must not melt. You can make this ahead of time, wrap well and freeze to use whenever you have a hankering for gluten-free puff pasty. Thaw in the refrigerator.

Makes 6 large or 12 small croissants

For the dough

250 ml/8 fl oz/1 cup warm whole milk or dairy-free substitute

125 ml/4 fl oz/½ cup warm double (heavy) cream or canned coconut milk

1 tbsp fast-action dried yeast (baking or active dry yeast)

50 g/2 oz/¼ cup sugar, plus 1 tsp

300 g/11 oz/17/8 cups sweet rice flour

90 g/3¼ oz/¾ cup sorghum flour

40 g/1½ oz/⅓ cup cornflour (cornstarch), plus extra for dusting

1 tbsp xanthan gum

1 tbsp salt

vegetable oil, for oiling

For the butter packet

225 g/8 oz/1 cup cold butter or dairy-free substitute, cut into cubes

3½ tsp white rice flour

1 tbsp sorghum flour

For the egg wash

1 medium (large) egg

1 tbsp double (heavy) cream or water

For the dough, stir the milk and cream together. Sprinkle the yeast and the 1 teaspoon sugar over the mixture and leave for 5–10 minutes until foamy.

Whisk all the dry ingredients, except the salt, together, then add the milk mixture with the salt and remaining sugar. Using the paddle attachment on a heavy-duty mixer, beat at medium-high speed for 3 minutes until a dough forms.

Place the dough in a lightly oiled bowl, cover with oiled plastic wrap and leave to rise for 30 minutes.

Gently fold the dough once and put back in the bowl. Cover and chill for at least 2 hours, or up to overnight.

To make the butter packet, put the cold butter cubes in a heavy-duty stand mixer fitted with the paddle attachment and sprinkle with the flours, then beat on low speed until blended. Once blended, but still cold, form into a 23 x 23 cm/9 x 9 inch square. Wrap in plastic wrap and chill until the dough has finished resting.

When the dough is ready (when chilled completely through), let the butter packet reach about 16°C/60°F, but still chilled and pliable.

Roll out the chilled dough into a 31 x 31 cm/12½ x 12½ inch square. Place the butter packet diagonally in the centre of the dough, then use the back of a butter knife to mark the dough at the corners of the butter. Remove the butter packet and roll out the corners a little, forming flaps where the marks are. Place the butter packet back on the dough and moisten the flaps slightly. Bring the flaps around the butter packet and overlay them slightly, sealing the edges enclosing the butter packet. Wrap in plastic wrap and chill for 30 minutes.

.

First Turn: place the dough seam-side up on a cold work surface or pastry board lightly dusted with cornflour (cornstarch). Gently roll the dough into a long rectangle about 8 cm/20 inches long and 18 cm/7 inches wide. Brush off the flour from the dough's surface and fold into thirds. Wrap the folded dough in plastic wrap and chill for 40 minutes.

Keep track on paper how many turns you have made. You can go as few as four turns, but I find six gives the best result. Sometimes the dough will only 'allow' you to do five turns before starting to crack and leak butter. If that is the case, stop at the fifth turn.

Second through sixth turns: repeat as the first turn, being sure to turn the dough occasionally to keep the seams and edges even. If liked, wrap the dough well and freeze for when you need gluten-free puff pastry, or continue to make croissants.

To shape the croissants

Preheat the oven to 220°C/425°F/Gas Mark 7. Lightly dust a cold counter with cornflour (cornstarch). Roll out the dough to a 50 x 18 cm/20 x 7 inch rectangle, trimming and saving some dough scraps for the inner part of the croissants. Then, using a knife or pizza cutter, cut into six or 12 triangles, depending on whether you want small or large croissants.

Gently stretch a triangle until it is a third longer than its original length. Place a piece of scrap dough in the centre and fold the long edge of the triangle over the scrap to enclose it. With the point formed by the two short sides of the triangle facing you, roll the dough towards you, gently moving your hands down out to the sides. Curve the pointed ends of the rolled croissant to form the traditional shape and place on a baking sheet. Repeat with the remaining dough.

For the egg wash, beat the egg and cream together, then use to brush over the croissants.

Put a few ice cubes in a tray and place in the oven with the croissants. Lower the oven temperature to 200°C/400°F/Gas Mark 6. After 10 minutes, rotate the baking sheet. Reduce the oven temperature to 190°C/375°F/Gas Mark 5 and bake for a further 8–10 minutes until the croissants are a deep golden brown. Transfer to a wire rack and cool for 30 minutes before serving.

PUMPKIN SEED BREAD

This loaf is packed with seeds for a nutty, hearty bread that toasts up beautifully.

Makes 1 loaf/ serves 8-10

50 g/2 oz/½ cup millet flakes

50 ml/2 fl oz/¼ cup boiling water

vegetable oil, for oiling

250 ml/8 fl oz/1 cup warm water

2¼ tsp fast-action dried yeast (baking or active dry yeast)

1 tsp apple cider vinegar

1 tsp light brown sugar

135 g/4¾ oz/1 cup finely ground brown rice flour, plus extra for sprinkling (optional)

85 g/3 oz/⅔ cup quinoa flour

60 g/2¼ oz/½ cup buckwheat flour

50 g/2 oz/½ cup tapioca flour (tapioca starch)

65 g/2½ oz/⅓ cup potato starch (*not* flour)

2 tsp xanthan gum

2 tsp salt

2 medium (large) eggs

2 tbsp honey

35g/1¼ oz/¼ cup pumpkin seeds, plus extra for sprinkling

2 tbsp sesame seeds, plus extra for sprinkling

Stir the millet and boiling water together in a small bowl and set aside for 10–15 minutes. Oil a 900 g/2 lb loaf pan.

Whisk the warm water, yeast, vinegar and sugar together in a heavy-duty stand mixer. Leave for 10 minutes until foamy.

Whisk all the flours, xanthan gum and salt together in a bowl. Add the eggs and honey to the wet ingredients and mix well.

Add the softened millet to the dry ingredients, then add to the wet ingredients, mix well, then beat on medium-high speed for 3 minutes. Stir in the seeds.

Spoon the dough into the prepared pan and smooth the surface. Press extra pumpkin and sesame seeds into the surface and sprinkle a little brown rice flour across the top, if liked. Loosely cover the surface with oiled plastic wrap and leave in a warm place to rise for about 1 hour until roughly doubled in size. Do not let the dough go over the rim of the pan.

Preheat the oven to 180°C/350°F/Gas Mark 4. Remove the plastic wrap and bake the bread for 45–55 minutes until browned and cooked through. Leave in the pan for 5 minutes before removing to a wire rack to cool.

SEEDED HONEY BREAD

A lightly sweet bread infused with honey and whole gluten-free grains.

Makes 1 loaf / serves 8–10

vegetable oil, for oiling

2 tbsp chia seeds

3 tbsp boiling water

175 ml/6 fl oz/¾ cup warm water

1 tsp granulated sugar

4 tsp fast-action dried yeast (baking or active dry yeast)

135 g/4¾ oz/1 cup brown rice flour, plus extra for dusting

125 g/4 oz/1 cup quinoa flour

50 g/2 oz/½ cup ground almonds

100 g/3½ oz/½ cup potato starch (*not* flour)

2 tsp salt

1 tbsp sesame seeds

2 tbsp pumpkin seeds

1 tbsp hemp seeds (hemp hearts)

2 medium (large) eggs

3 tbsp honey

extra sesame, pumpkin and hemp seeds for sprinkling (optional)

Oil a 900 g/2 lb loaf pan.

Stir the chia seeds and the 3 tablespoons boiling water together in a bowl and set aside.

In another bowl, combine the 175 ml/6 fl oz/¾ cup warm water and sugar. Sprinkle the yeast over the mixture and leave to stand for 5–10 minutes until foamy, then stir to combine.

Mix the flours, ground almonds, potato starch, salt, and seeds in a heavy-duty stand mixer fitted with a paddle attachment. While beating, slowly add the yeast mixture, eggs, soaked chia seed mixture and honey and beat until incorporated, then once everything has been added, beat on medium-high speed for 2 minutes.

Scoop the dough into the prepared loaf pan and sprinkle any extra seeds on top, if liked. Dust the top lightly with brown rice flour, then cover with oiled plastic wrap and let the dough rise at room temperature for about 45 minutes until doubled in size.

Preheat the oven to 200°C/400°F/Gas Mark 6.

Remove the plastic wrap and bake the bread for 10 minutes, then lower the oven temperature to 180°C/350°F/Gas Mark 4 and bake for a further 30 minutes until the loaf is golden brown.

Leave to cool in the pan for 5 minutes, then remove and cool on a wire rack.

CURRIED MILLET & AMARANTH BREAD

This makes a wonderful chicken sandwich with a little mango chutney smeared on the bread.

Makes 1 loaf / serves 8–10

vegetable oil, for oiling and spritzing

300 ml/10 fl oz/1¼ cups warm water

3 medium (large) eggs

50 ml/2 fl oz/¼ cup vegetable oil

1 tsp apple cider vinegar

60 g/2¼ oz/½ cup amaranth flour

125 g/4 oz/1 cup millet flour

165 g/5½ oz/1½ cups tapioca flour (starch)

135 g/4¾ oz/1 cup brown rice flour

65 g/2½ oz/⅔ cup ground almonds

2 tsp xanthan gum

1 tsp salt

1½ tbsp ground flaxseed, preferably golden flaxseed

1½ tbsp fast-action dried yeast (baking or active dry yeast)

35 g/1¼ oz/¼ cup light brown sugar

1 tbsp curry powder

40 g/1½ oz/¼ cup chopped onion, sautéed until translucent (optional)

Oil a 900 g/2 lb loaf pan.

Mix the warm water, eggs, oil and vinegar together in a heavy-duty stand mixer fitted with the batter attachment.

Whisk the dry ingredients, except the onions, together in a bowl. Add the dry ingredients to the wet ingredients and stir together until combined, then beat on medium-high speed for 3 minutes. Stir in the onions.

Spoon the batter into the prepared loaf pan and smooth the top. Spritz the top with oil and cover with oiled plastic wrap. Leave to rise for about 45 minutes until the batter is at the edge of the pan, but doesn't go over the rim.

Preheat the oven to 200°C/400°F/Gas Mark 6.

Bake the bread for 10 minutes, then tent with foil. Lower the oven temperature to 190°C/375°F/Gas Mark 5 and bake for a further 35–40 minutes. Leave to cool in the pan for 5 minutes before removing and cooling on a wire rack.

CARROT LOAF CAKE WITH CINNAMON

Double the recipe and top with cream cheese frosting for a carrot cake delight.

Makes 1 loaf / serves 10

125 ml/4 fl oz/½ cup vegetable oil, plus extra for oiling

150 g/5 oz/1 cup soft brown sugar

2 medium (large) eggs

50 g/2 oz/packed ½ cup finely grated carrots

200 g/7 oz/1½ cups Bean Flour Blend (*see* page 70)

¾ tsp xanthan gum

1 tsp ground cinnamon

1 tsp bicarbonate of soda (baking soda)

½ tsp salt

75 g/3 oz/½ cup raisins or toasted nuts (optional)

Preheat the oven to 180°C/350°F/Gas Mark 4. Oil a 900 g/2 lb loaf pan.

Cream the sugar and oil together in a bowl. Beat in the eggs, then add the carrots. Combine the dry ingredients in another bowl, then add to the sugar mixture with the raisins, if using. Mix until well blended.

Pour the batter into the prepared loaf pan and smooth the top. Bake for 30–40 minutes until a cocktail stick (toothpick) inserted into the centre comes out clean. Cool before eating.

RAISIN WHIRLS

These sweet breakfast spirals make a wonderful start to the day!

Makes 15 whirls

3 tbsp butter or dairy-free substitute, melted

3 tbsp granulated sugar

2 tbsp ground cinnamon

1 quantity Gluten-free Croissant dough, chilled (*see* page 97)

150 g/5 oz/1 cup raisins

1 medium (large) egg mixed with 1 tbsp water (optional)

sugar, for sprinkling (optional)

Preheat the oven to 220°C/425°F/Gas Mark 7. Line a baking sheet with baking parchment.

To make the filling, stir the butter, sugar and cinnamon together in a bowl.

Roll out the dough into a rectangle on plastic wrap. Brush with the butter mixture and sprinkle with the raisins. Roll up the dough using the plastic wrap to form a cylinder shape. Pinch the edge together to seal.

Cut the dough into 2 cm/¾ inch sections and place on the baking sheet. Brush the whirls with egg wash and sprinkle with sugar, if liked.

Place the whirls in the oven, then lower the oven temperature to 190°C/375°F/Gas Mark 5 and bake for 15–18 minutes until crisp and golden. Eat warm or leave to cool.

FLAXSEED ROLLS

These soft yet hearty rolls are a welcome sight at any meal.

Makes 12 rolls or 6 burger buns

1½ tsp unflavoured gelatine

3 tbsp water

250 ml/8 fl oz/1 cup warm milk or dairy-free milk substitute

2¼ tsp fast-action dried yeast (baking or active dry yeast)

1 tbsp granulated sugar

400 g/14 oz/3 cups Bean Flour Blend (see page 70)

3 tbsp brown sugar

2¼ tsp xanthan gum

½ tsp salt

3 large (extra large) eggs

50 g/2 oz/¼ cup softened butter, organic shortening or 3 tbsp coconut oil

1½ tsp cider vinegar

30 g/1 oz/¼ cup flaxseeds, preferably golden flaxseed

1 medium (large) egg mixed well with 1 tbsp water

Line a baking sheet with baking parchment.

Sprinkle the gelatine onto the water in a small bowl and set aside until the gelatine has absorbed all the water. Mix the gelatine into the warm milk, then add the yeast and the granulated sugar and set aside.

Mix the flour, brown sugar, xanthan gum and salt together in a heavy-duty stand mixer and blend well. Add the milk mixture, eggs, butter and vinegar. Mix at a low speed until blended, then add the flaxseed and mix at high speed for 3 minutes to form a dough.

Using very wet or oiled hands, divide the dough into 6 balls, about 3 tablespoons dough per ball. Place the dough balls evenly spaced onto the baking sheet. Cover with oiled plastic wrap and leave to rise for about 45 minutes–1 hour until almost doubled in size. Brush the buns with the egg wash, then using a knife, cut a 5 mm/¼ inch deep slash in the dough on each bun.

Preheat the oven to 190°C/375°F/Gas Mark 5.

Bake the buns for 25–30 minutes. Leave to cool on a wire rack.

Burger Buns

To make burger buns, omit the flaxseed and divide the dough into 6 balls. After rising, bake for 30–40 minutes until baked through. For a very dark crust, brush with egg wash twice before making the cuts in the buns, if liked.

FLATBREAD WITH SESAME SEEDS

While you can bake this bread the same day you mix it, it will have the best taste and texture if you let the dough rest in the refrigerator overnight.

Serves 8–10

400 ml/14 fl oz/1⅔ cups water, at room temperature

100 ml/3½ fl oz/⅓ cup olive oil, plus extra for oiling

2 medium (large) eggs

125 g/4 oz/1 cup sorghum or rice flour

110 g/3¾ oz/1 cup tapioca flour (tapioca starch)

100 g/3½ oz/½ cup potato starch (*not* flour)

40 g/1½ oz/¼ cup rice flour

50 g/2 oz/½ cup ground almonds

2 tbsp granulated sugar

2 tsp fast-action dried yeast (baking or active dry yeast)

3 tsp xanthan gum

1 tsp salt

For the topping

sea salt, for sprinkling

½ tbsp sesame seeds

Mix the water, oil and eggs together in a heavy-duty stand mixer until frothy.

Whisk the flours, ground almonds, sugar, yeast, xanthan gum and salt together in another bowl.

Add the dry ingredients to the wet ingredients and mix on low speed, scraping the sides of the bowl down as needed until blended, then blend on high speed for 3 minutes. Cover the bowl with plastic wrap and chill the dough overnight. It will rise in the refrigerator, so allow room for expansion.

The next day, let the dough come back to room temperature for 30 minutes.

Preheat the oven to 180°C/350°F/Gas Mark 4 and line a baking sheet with baking parchment.

Using well-oiled hands, spread and flatten the dough onto the baking parchment, then using your fingers, make dimples in the top of the dough. Sprinkle with sea salt and sesame seeds.

Leave the bread to rise at room temperature for 15 minutes, then bake for 30 minutes until golden and cooked through. Leave to cool on the baking sheet for 5 minutes before moving to a wire rack to cool.

GLUTEN-FREE BAGUETTE

Baguettes are endlessly versatile and they are one of the breads I make most often to round out a meal.

Makes 2 loaves

vegetable oil, for oiling

300 ml/10 fl oz/1¼ cups warm water, skimmed milk or dairy-free substitute

2 tbsp fast-action dried yeast (baking or active dry yeast)

1 tbsp granulated sugar

375 g/13 oz/1¾ cups potato starch (*not* flour)

125 g/4 oz/¾ cup plus 2 tbsp sorghum flour

85 g/3 oz/½ cup plus 2 tbsp tapioca flour (tapioca starch)

2 tsp xanthan gum

1 tsp salt

1 tbsp olive oil

1 medium (large) egg plus 1 egg white

2 tsp cider vinegar

1 medium (large) egg mixed well with 1 tbsp water

Oil a rimmed baking sheet or baguette bread pan. If using French bread or baguette pans, line the indentations with foil or baking parchment and oil the foil or parchment.

Mix the yeast and sugar into the warm water and set aside.

Whisk the all the flours, xanthan gum and salt together in a heavy-duty stand mixer. Add the yeast mixture, the olive oil, eggs and cider vinegar and using the paddle attachment, beat at a low speed, scraping down the sides of the bowl, if needed, until blended, then beat at a high speed for 2 minutes to form a dough.

Place the dough in a freezerproof bag, snip the corner and squeeze out half the dough into a thick line on the baking sheet or pan for one loaf. Repeat with the remaining dough. Using wet hands, smooth the dough into logs about 30–35 cm/12–14 inches long. At this point, you can brush with egg wash, if liked. Make three diagonal slashes in the dough about 5 mm/¼ inch deep.

Place the baking sheet or pan on the middle rack in a *cold* oven and set the oven to 220°C/425°F/Gas Mark 7. Bake for 30–35 minutes until the two loaves until nicely browned.

Leave the bread to cool before slicing.

QUICHES, TARTS & PIZZAS

MINI QUICHES LORRAINES

These mini quiches make a lovely brunch dish. Probably the most famous quiche, Quiche Lorraine is named for its region of origin. The classic recipe contains no cheese, so feel free to skip the cheese, if liked.

Serves 6

1 quantity Shortcrust Pastry dough (*see* page 76)

gluten-free flour, for dusting

65 g/2½ oz/½ cup chopped ham or cooked crumbled bacon

40 g/1½ oz/¼ cup chopped onion

100 g/3½ oz/1 cup grated Swiss/Emmental or Gouda cheese or dairy-free substitute

4 medium (large) eggs

500 ml/18 fl oz/2 cups single cream (half-and-half) or canned unsweetened coconut milk

½ tsp salt

¼ tsp freshly ground black pepper

Roll out the dough on a lightly floured work surface to 5 mm/¼ inch thick. Cut out 6 circles to fit six mini tart pans, then press the dough circles onto the bottom and up the sides of the pans. Trim the dough flush with the top edge of the pans. Prick the bottoms all over with a fork and transfer to a rimmed baking sheet. Freeze until firm while the oven is preheating.

Preheat the oven to 190°C/375°F/Gas Mark 5. Remove the tart cases (shells) from the freezer and divide the ham and onion equally between them. Top with the cheese.

Whisk the eggs, cream, salt and pepper together in a bowl until well incorporated, then pour the mixture into the tart cases. Place in the oven and lower the oven temperature to 160°C/325°F/Gas Mark 3. Bake for 30–35 minutes until the filling is set. Cool for 10 minutes before serving.

MARGHERITA PIZZA

This pizza shows off the colours of the Italian flag with red tomatoes, white mozzarella and green basil.

Serves 6

For the pizza crust

1½ tbsp olive oil, plus extra for oiling and drizzling

100 g/3½ oz/¾ cup brown rice flour

30 g/1 oz/¼ cup amaranth flour

110 g/3¾ oz/1 cup tapioca flour (tapioca starch)

1½ tsp xanthan gum

½ tsp salt

1 tbsp easy-blend dried (active dry) yeast

½ tbsp granulated sugar

175 ml/6 fl oz/¾ cup warm water

2 egg whites at room temperature

For the toppings

125 ml/4 fl oz/½ cup ready-made marinara sauce

335 g/11¾ oz/3 cups grated mozzarella cheese or dairy-free substitute

185 g/6½ oz/¾ cup canned chopped tomatoes, drained, or chopped fresh tomatoes

8 basil leaves, thinly sliced

1 tbsp very finely chopped oregano or 1 tsp dried oregano

½ tsp crushed dried chili (pepper) flakes (optional)

⅛ tsp freshly ground black pepper

To make the pizza crust, preheat the oven to 200°C/400°F/Gas Mark 6. Oil a 33 cm/13 inch pizza pan or baking sheet and set aside.

Combine the flours, xanthan gum, salt, yeast and sugar in a heavy-duty stand mixer.

Combine the warm water and oil in a jug, then add to the dry ingredients with the egg whites and mix well. Beat on high speed for 4 minutes until a dough forms.

Scoop the dough onto the pizza pan. Drizzle 1 tablespoon olive oil over your hand and the dough, then pat the dough out into a circular shape.

To make the pizza, spread the marinara sauce over the dough until it is 1 cm/½ inch from the edge. Top with the remaining ingredients. Bake for 20 minutes, or until the crust is golden and the cheese is melted.

GARDEN QUICHE

This is a beautiful quiche to make when we're at the height of the growing season and vegetables are plentiful.

Serves 8

½ quantity Shortcrust Pastry dough (*see* page 76)

gluten-free flour, for dusting

1 tbsp vegetable oil

1 sweet onion, peeled and diced

1 celery stalk, diced

1 small leek, trimmed and thinly sliced

2 courgettes (zucchini), one sliced into 5 mm/¼ inch rounds
    and one coarsely grated

4 medium (large) eggs

250 ml/8 fl oz/1 cup sour cream or dairy-free substitute

125 ml/4 fl oz/½ cup milk or dairy-free substitute

½ tsp ground nutmeg

85 g/3 oz/¾ cup grated Gruyère or Gouda cheese, or dairy-free substitute

90 g/3¼ oz/⅓ cup chèvre, crumbled

1 tomato, such as Roma, sliced into rounds

3 tsp dried, or 3 tbsp fresh, dill or oregano, for sprinkling

salt and freshly ground black pepper

Preheat the oven to 180°C/350°F/Gas Mark 4. Roll out the dough on a lightly floured work surface and use to line a 23 cm/9 inch pie pan. Trim and shape the pastry edge as desired.

Prick the bottom of the dough with a fork, then line with baking parchment and fill with baking or dried beans. Bake for 20 minutes, then remove the parchment and beans. Set aside.

For the quiche, heat the oil in a frying pan over a medium heat and fry the onion, celery and leek for 5–7 minutes until the onion is translucent. Add all the courgette (zucchini) and cook until the courgette rounds are tender but still retain their shape, about 5–7 minutes. Take the pan off the heat and set aside.

Beat the eggs, sour cream, milk and nutmeg together until combined. Remove the courgette rounds from the pan and set aside. Add the remaining cooked vegetables and both cheeses to the egg mixture and fold together. Pour into the pastry case (shell). Arrange the courgette rounds and the tomato on top. Sprinkle with dill, season and bake for 30–40 minutes until the egg is set.

MUSHROOM, LEEK & CHEESE TART

A lovely tart for the spring table.

Serves 8

½ quantity Shortcrust Pastry dough (*see* page 76)

gluten-free flour, for dusting

1 tbsp olive oil

1 leek, trimmed and thinly sliced

150 g/5 oz/2 cups mushrooms, sliced

½ tsp salt

½ tsp freshly ground pepper

4 medium (large) eggs

250 ml/8 fl oz/1 cup milk or dairy-free unsweetened substitute

2 tsp thyme leaves

80 g/3 oz/¾ cup grated Swiss/Emmental cheese or dairy-free substitute

Preheat the oven to 180°C/350°F/Gas Mark 4. Roll out the dough on a lightly floured work surface and use to line a 23 cm/9 inch pie pan. Trim and shape the pastry edge as desired. Prick the bottom of the dough with a fork, then line with baking parchment and fill with baking or dried beans. Bake for 20 minutes, then remove the parchment and beans. Set aside.

Heat the oil in a frying pan over a medium-high heat. Add the leek and mushrooms, season with the salt and pepper and cook for 8–10 minutes until the leeks are tender, the mushrooms are golden and no liquid remains in the pan.

Whisk the eggs, milk and thyme together. Sprinkle 50 g/2 oz/½ cup cheese over the bottom of the case (shell), then spread the vegetable mixture over the top. Sprinkle with the remaining cheese and pour in the egg mixture. Bake for 30–40 minutes until the egg is set.

THAI CHICKEN PIZZA

This is a fun twist on the usual pizza and is a family favourite. I often add diced red sweet (bell) pepper to the toppings as well.

Serves 6

1 quantity pizza crust ingredients (*see* page 120)

For the sauce

3 tbsp natural peanut butter

1½ tbsp gluten-free soy sauce

1½ tbsp water

1½ tbsp brown sugar

1 tsp rice vinegar

½ tsp very finely chopped garlic

¼ tsp crushed dried chili (pepper) flakes

For the toppings

1 tbsp olive oil

1 skinless, boneless chicken breast, thinly sliced

2 tbsp gluten-free soy sauce

125 g/4 oz/1 cup grated mozzarella cheese or dairy-free substitute

20 g/¾ oz/¼ cup beansprouts

2 medium spring onions (scallions), thinly sliced

3 tbsp chopped coriander (cilantro)

1½ tbsp chopped roasted peanuts

Preheat the oven to 200°C/400°F/Gas Mark 6.

Mix all the sauce ingredients together in a small pan. Heat slightly if needed to create a smooth, spreadable sauce. Set aside.

To cook the chicken, heat the oil in a frying pan and fry the chicken with the soy sauce until the chicken is cooked through. Set aside.

Make the pizza dough and shape according to the instructions on page 120. Spread the pizza dough with the sauce until it is 1 cm/½ inch from the edge. Top the pizza with the cheese, chicken, beansprouts and onions.

Bake for 20 minutes until the crust is golden and the pizza is cooked. Sprinkle with coriander (cilantro) and peanuts.

QUINOA & COURGETTE CAKES

These cakes can be cooked in a mould (as shown), baked in a well-oiled mini muffin pan or made into patties and fried in an oiled pan depending on how you would like to serve them.

Serves 4

250 ml/8 fl oz/1 cup gluten-free chicken or vegetable stock

85 g/3 oz/½ cup quinoa, well rinsed

olive oil, for cooking

1 courgette (zucchini), grated or diced

60 g/2¼ oz/⅔ cup grated Parmesan or dairy-free substitute

¼ tsp freshly ground black pepper

1 egg, beaten

1 egg white

Stir the stock and quinoa together in a saucepan and bring to the boil. Reduce the heat, cover and simmer until all the stock is absorbed. Turn off the heat and keep covered for 5–10 minutes. Fluff the quinoa with a fork and leave to cool.

Preheat the oven to 180°C/350°F/Gas Mark 4. Oil a baking sheet and four ring moulds and set the ring moulds on the baking sheet.

Squeeze any excess moisture from the courgette (zucchini) and mix with the quinoa, Parmesan and black pepper. Add the beaten egg and egg white and mix together thoroughly.

Spoon the mixture into the ring moulds, pressing down with damp hands until the top is even, then brush lightly with oil. Bake for 20–25 minutes until lightly golden. Cool slightly, then gently ease the cakes out of the moulds.

LIGHT MEALS & SIDES

ROASTED PUMPKIN SOUP

Roasted pumpkin soup is comforting on a cool autumn evening, yet would look lovely as a special dinner. Sprinkle with golden flaxseed, roasted pumpkin seeds or crisp crumbled bacon.

Serves 4-6

4 tbsp olive oil

1.8 kg/4 lb small pumpkin, cut in half and deseeded, then cut in half again

1 large onion, peeled and chopped

4 garlic cloves, peeled and very finely chopped

½ tsp salt

½ tsp ground cinnamon

¼ tsp ground nutmeg

⅛ tsp cloves

¼ tsp freshly ground black pepper

dash cayenne pepper (optional)

1 litre/1¾ pints/4 cups gluten-free chicken or vegetable stock

120 ml/4 fl oz/½ cup canned coconut milk, or dairy cream

2 tbsp maple syrup or honey (optional)

Preheat the oven to 220°C/425°F/Gas Mark 7 and line a baking sheet with baking parchment. Brush 1 tablespoon oil over the pumpkin and place the quarters, cut sides down, onto the baking sheet. Roast for 35 minutes, or until the flesh is easily pierced through with a fork. Cool for a few minutes.

Heat the remaining oil in a pan or casserole dish over a medium-high heat and fry the onion and garlic for 5–7 minutes until the onion is translucent. Remove the skin from the pumpkin and discard.

When the onion is translucent, add the pumpkin, salt, spices, pepper and cayenne, if using. Pour in the stock. Bring to the boil, then reduce the heat and simmer for 10–15 minutes, breaking up the pumpkin and stirring occasionally.

Add the coconut milk and maple syrup, then use a stick or immersion blender to purée the soup until smooth. Season to taste. Alternatively, working in batches, purée the soup in a blender. Taste and adjust the seasoning, if necessary, and serve.

AVOCADO & LIME HUMMUS

This hummus is a cross between guacamole and hummus. It makes a great dip for a gathering or a lovely addition to a light lunch.

Serves 6-8

425 g/15 oz/1⅔ cups canned chickpeas, drained and rinsed

1 ripe avocado, stoned and peeled

5 g/⅛ oz/¼ cup very finely chopped coriander (cilantro)

3 tbsp tahini

1–2 garlic cloves, peeled and very finely chopped

juice of 1 lime

½ tsp ground coriander

100–125 ml/3½–4 fl oz/⅓–½ cup water

½ tsp salt

freshly ground black pepper

Combine all the ingredients, except the water and salt and pepper, in a food processor and process until smooth, adding the water a little at a time until the desired texture is reached. Season to taste.

BEETROOT HUMMUS

This delicious hummus gets its glorious colour and healthy boost of vitamins from the beetroot.

Serves 6–8

3 small beetroot, about 150 g/5 oz, well scrubbed

2–4 tbsp olive oil, plus extra for drizzling

salt

425 g/15 oz/1⅔ cups canned chickpeas, rinsed and drained

juice of 1 lemon

2 tbsp tahini

1–2 garlic cloves, peeled and very finely chopped

½ tsp smoked paprika

To garnish

1 tbsp chopped walnuts

1 tbsp very finely chopped dill

Preheat the oven to 220°C/425°F/Gas Mark 7.

Place the beetroot on a sheet of foil, add a drizzle of oil, sprinkle with salt, then wrap the foil loosely around the beetroot. Roast for 45–60 minutes until tender. Cool, then peel the skins and dice the beetroot.

Combine the beetroot with the remaining ingredients, except the oil, in a food processor. Purée until smooth, drizzling in the oil until the hummus is the desired consistency.

Sprinkle with walnuts and dill.

CHICKEN & POMEGRANATE PILAF

This mouthwatering pilaf is a great way to use up leftover chicken. For a change, use cooked turkey or pork.

Serves 4–6

25 g/1 oz/2 tbsp/¼ stick butter or coconut oil

1 small onion, very finely chopped

1 medium carrot, peeled and cut into matchsticks

275 g/10 oz/1½ cups long-grain rice

1 garlic clove, peeled and very finely chopped

500 ml/18 fl oz/2 cups gluten-free chicken stock

250 ml/8 fl oz/1 cup water

1 tsp salt

½ tsp ground black pepper

90 g/3¼ oz/½ cup pomegranate seeds

2 tbsp chopped flat-leaf parsley

Heat the butter in a saucepan and fry the onion and carrot over a medium heat for 5–7 minutes until the onion is translucent. Add the rice and garlic and fry for 1 minute to coat the rice in the oil.

Add the stock, water, salt and pepper and bring to a simmer. Reduce the heat to very low, cover and cook for 15–18 minutes until the rice is cooked. Stir in half the pomegranate seeds.

Sprinkle with the remaining pomegranate seeds and parsley.

CAULIFLOWER COUSCOUS

This is a fun, grain-free dish that comes together fast. Once you have pulsed the cauliflower and sautéed it, it can be used in any dish instead of couscous.

Serves 4

1 head cauliflower, trimmed and divided into florets

4 tbsp olive oil or coconut oil

½ medium shallot, peeled

1 garlic clove, peeled and very finely chopped

50 g/2 oz/⅓ cup raisins

20 g/¾ oz/⅓ cup chopped flat-leaf parsley

very finely chopped zest and juice of 1 lemon

1 tsp sea salt

freshly ground black pepper

90 g/3¼ oz/½ cup pomegranate seeds

50 g/2 oz/⅓ cup pumpkin seeds

Pulse the cauliflower in a food processor until it resembles couscous.

Heat 1 tablespoon oil in a frying pan and fry the cauliflower, shallot and garlic for 7–10 minutes until the cauliflower is tender. Stir in the raisins and take off the heat.

Whisk the remaining oil, parsley, lemon zest and juice, salt and pepper together in a bowl, then pour over the cauliflower. Add half the pomegranate seeds and toss together.

Top with the remaining pomegranate seeds and pumpkin seeds.

BUCKWHEAT GNOCCHI

Gnocchi are a cross between pasta and a dumpling. Buckwheat flour gives these a slightly nutty flavour that complements many different sauces.

Serves 4

900 g/2 lb baking potatoes, such as Russet, scrubbed clean
125 g/4 oz/1 cup buckwheat flour, plus extra for dusting
1 tbsp salt
1 large egg, beaten

Preheat the oven to 220°C/425°F/Gas Mark 7.

Roast the potatoes for 40–50 minutes until done. Cool for a few minutes, then cut each potato in half, scoop out the flesh and place it in a potato ricer. Spread out the potato where you will knead the pasta, and leave the potato to cool to room temperature.

Add the flour and salt to the potato and mix well. Create a well in the centre, add the egg and knead together into a sticky dough, working quickly and adding as little flour as possible.

Bring a small pan of water to the boil. Take a small piece of dough, about the size of a grape, and drop it into the boiling water. It will cook for about 1 minute, then should rise to the surface. Cook for a further minute, then remove with a slotted spoon. If, rather than sink and then rise, it breaks apart, add a little more flour to the dough and knead again. Once you get a test one that sinks then rises without falling apart, you are ready to shape the remaining dough. The test gnocchi should be cooked through, but still soft and light.

Lightly dust the work surface with flour and lightly flour a baking pan. Divide the dough into six equal-size pieces. Place one of the pieces on the floured surface, then using the palms of your hands, roll the piece out into a 1 cm/½ inch thick log, about 30 cm/12 inches long. Cut the log into 2.5 cm/1 inch lengths.

To shape the gnocchi, position a 2.5 cm/1 inch dough segment on the back of a fork and slowly roll the dough down the length of the fork tines while pressing lightly on the dough with your thumb at the same time to form a shallow indentation in the back of the gnocchi. Place the gnocchi onto the prepared baking pan and repeat with the remaining dough.

Bring a large pan of salted water to the boil. Add the gnocchi in small batches. Once they have risen to the top, cook for a further minute, then scoop them out with a slotted spoon and lay them on a baking sheet to cool. At this point, they are ready to use.

FALAFEL

These falafel are delicious served with a cucumber yogurt sauce, hummus with a large tray of vegetables for dipping and tomatoes still warm from the vine.

Serves 6-8

400 g/14 oz/2 cups dried chickpeas

1 small onion, peeled and quartered

3 garlic cloves, peeled and smashed

15 g/½ oz/1 packed cup coriander (cilantro) leaves

60 g/2¼ oz/1 packed cup flat-leaf parsley leaves

finely grated zest of 1 large lemon

1 tbsp ground cumin

1½ tsp salt

½ tsp ground black pepper

¼ tsp cayenne pepper

2–4 tbsp chickpea flour (optional)

½ tsp bicarbonate of soda (baking soda) (optional)

vegetable oil, for frying

coarse salt, for sprinkling

Put the chickpeas in a large bowl and fill with enough water to cover them to a depth of 7.5 cm/3 inches. Cover the bowl with plastic wrap and soak for 24 hours, checking a few times during soaking to see if you need to add more water. Drain and rinse well.

Place the chickpeas, onion, garlic, coriander (cilantro), parsley, lemon zest, cumin, salt, pepper and cayenne into a food processor and alternate between pulsing and blending, stopping frequently to scrape down the sides of the bowl, until the mixture is uniform in size and still slightly grainy in texture. Taste and adjust the seasoning if necessary.

Roll a small amount of the mixture into a walnut-size ball with your hands. The mixture should hold together and not fall apart. If it seems too wet, sprinkle with a small amount of flour, no more than 1 tablespoon at a time. Once the texture is correct, sprinkle the bicarbonate of soda (baking soda) over the mixture and stir until combined. Continue rolling the remaining batter into uniform-size balls, placing them on a baking sheet.

Pour the oil into a casserole dish or a large, high-sided frying pan to a depth of 7.5 cm/3 inches. Place a cook's thermometer into the oil and heat over a medium-high heat until the temperature reaches 182–190°C/360–375°F. When the oil is at the correct temperature, fry a test falafel. The oil should bubble up and sizzle all around it. The falafel should stay together in one piece and not break apart. It should take 1½–2 minutes to deep-fry until golden brown. If the falafel is not completely submerged flip over and cook the other side until it's browned all over. Remove the cooked falafel from the oil and drain on a platter lined with paper towels. Sprinkle with coarse salt while it is still hot. Fry the remaining falafel in batches, being careful to not overcrowd the pan.

STUFFED PEPPERS WITH QUINOA & WALNUTS

I love stuffed peppers with all sorts of fillings. This vegan recipe can be used as a main dish or as a side.

Serves 4

4 large red (bell) peppers

300 ml/10 fl oz/1¼ cups gluten-free vegetable stock

175 g/6 oz/1 cup quinoa, rinsed and drained

425 g/15 oz/1¾ cups canned diced tomatoes, drained

5 g/⅛ oz/¼ cup very finely chopped basil

60 g/2¼ oz/½ cup chopped walnuts

1 tbsp olive oil

1 onion, peeled and diced

2 garlic cloves, peeled and very finely chopped

3 tbsp very finely chopped parsley

1 tbsp Italian seasoning

salt and freshly ground black pepper

Preheat the oven to 180°C/350°F/Gas Mark 4 and line a baking dish with baking parchment. Cut the tops off the peppers and reserve, then remove the seeds and scrape out the flesh with a spoon. Set the peppers aside.

Mix the stock, quinoa, tomatoes and half of the basil together in a saucepan and bring to the boil. Reduce the heat to the lowest setting, cover with a lid and simmer for 15 minutes until the liquid is absorbed.

Meanwhile, toast the walnuts in a pan for a few minutes, being careful not to let them scorch. Transfer to a large bowl and set aside.

Heat the oil in a frying pan over a medium heat and fry the onion and garlic for 5–7 minutes until the onion is translucent. Add to the bowl with the walnuts.

When the quinoa is ready, add it to the bowl together with the parsley and Italian seasoning. Season and mix together thoroughly.

Divide the quinoa mixture between the peppers, then put the tops back and arrange them upright in the dish. Cover with foil and bake for 45 minutes–1 hour until the peppers are tender.

VEGGIE FRITTATA WITH DILL

Frittatas are normally cooked in an ovenproof frying pan, but not everyone has one, so I have included instructions on how to make a frittata without one. If you do have an ovenproof pan, after frying the veggies, pour the egg mixture into the pan and pop in the oven to cook.

Serves 4

1–2 tbsp olive oil, plus extra for oiling

1 small carrot, peeled and very thinly sliced

1 bunch asparagus, ends trimmed and chopped

130 g/4½ oz/1 cup cooked peas or frozen peas, thawed

8 medium (large) eggs, lightly whisked

4 tbsp grated Parmesan

salt and freshly ground black pepper

2 tbsp dill leaves, to serve

Preheat the oven to 200°C/400°F/Gas Mark 6. Oil a 23 cm/9 inch round cake pan.

Heat the oil in a frying pan over a medium-high heat and fry the carrot and asparagus for 5–7 minutes until tender. Add the peas and heat through, then place the vegetables into the cake pan.

Beat the eggs, Parmesan and salt and pepper together in a bowl.

Pour the egg mixture into the pan and bake in the oven for 12–15 minutes until the eggs are set. Cool for 5 minutes, then slice into wedges. Sprinkle with dill.

Main Meals

PUMPKIN RISOTTO

This recipe is also delicious with butternut squash instead of pumpkin.

Serves 4

50 ml/2 fl oz/¼ cup olive oil

60 g/2¼ oz/½ cup diced pumpkin, plus 125 g/4 oz/½ cup puréed cooked pumpkin

6 sage leaves

1 large shallot, peeled and diced

2 garlic cloves, peeled and very finely chopped

200 g/7 oz/1 cup arborio rice

125 ml/4 fl oz/½ cup dry white wine

750 ml/1¼ pints/3 cups gluten-free chicken or vegetable stock, heated

25 g/1 oz/¼ cup grated Parmesan or dairy-free alternative

25 g/1 oz/2 tbsp/¼ stick butter or 1 tbsp coconut oil

¼ tsp grated nutmeg; salt and freshly ground black pepper

Heat 1 tablespoon oil in a frying pan and fry the diced pumpkin for 10–15 minutes until softened. Set aside. Heat the remaining oil and quickly fry the sage for a few seconds. Remove with a slotted spoon and set aside.

Add the shallot to the sage oil and sauté until translucent. Add the garlic and fry for 1 minute. Add the rice and stir to coat with the oil. Add the wine and simmer for 3–5 minutes until all the liquid is absorbed. Spoon 125 ml/4 fl oz/½ cup of the warm stock into the rice and simmer, stirring occasionally, until the stock is absorbed. Repeat, adding 125 ml/4 fl oz/½ cup of stock at a time, until the rice is cooked but still firm, 20–25 minutes total.

Stir in the pumpkin purée, Parmesan, butter or coconut oil, nutmeg, salt and pepper. Top with the diced pumpkin and sage.

SWEET & SOUR CHICKEN

If you like veggies in your sweet and sour, sauté a chopped sweet red (bell) pepper, green pepper and/or half an onion. Add 165 g/5¾ oz/1 cup chopped pineapple for a sweet twist.

Serves 4

For the sauce

100 ml/3½ fl oz/⅓ cup gluten-free soy sauce

50 ml/2 fl oz/¼ cup gluten-free chicken stock

2 tbsp tomato purée (paste)

3 tbsp honey or soft brown sugar

2 tbsp rice vinegar

¼ tsp toasted sesame oil

2 garlic cloves, peeled and very finely chopped

½ tsp finely grated ginger

3 tbsp water

2 tbsp cornflour (cornstarch)

For the chicken

4 skinless, boneless chicken breasts, cut into 2.5 cm/1 inch pieces

40 g/1½ oz/⅓ cup cornflour (cornstarch)

2–3 tbsp vegetable oil, for cooking

For the sauce, combine all the ingredients, except the water and cornflour (cornstarch), in a saucepan. Stir and bring to the boil. Meanwhile, whisk the water and cornflour together in a small bowl to a paste, then add to the pan and stir until thickened. Keep warm.

For the chicken, place the chicken and cornflour in a zip-lock freezer bag. Seal and shake until the chicken is coated.

Heat some oil in a frying pan over a medium-high heat. Working in batches, fry the chicken until it is browned on all sides and cooked through. Add the sauce and stir to coat well. Serve warm.

ROAST TURKEY SANDWICH
with Cucumber Relish

This sandwich is a wonderful way to use up leftover turkey. However, you can enjoy it any time by cooking a turkey breast fillet to use for the filling. The cucumber relish makes about 300 ml/10 fl oz/1¼ cups.

Serves 4–6

For the cucumber relish

450 g/1 lb seedless cucumbers, diced

¼ small onion, peeled and very finely chopped

1 tbsp sea salt

200 ml/7 fl oz/¾ cup white wine vinegar

50 g/2 oz/¼ cup granulated sugar

1 tsp mustard seeds

½ tsp celery seeds

¼ tsp ground turmeric

For the turkey

1½ tsp salt

1 tsp ground dried sage

½ tsp ground dried rosemary

½ tsp dried thyme

½ tsp ground black pepper

1 tbsp olive oil

70–900 g/1½–2 lb unseasoned turkey breast fillet (tenderloin)

For the sandwich

4–6 Burger Buns (see page 111), scattered with sesame seeds prior to baking, if liked

1 quantity Mustard (see page 196)

For the relish, mix the cucumbers, onion and salt in a colander and leave for 30 minutes. Transfer the cucumbers to a clean tea (dish) towel and, using your hands, squeeze to remove as much moisture as possible.

Combine the cucumber mixture with the remaining ingredients in a pan and simmer, stirring occasionally, for 4–6 minutes until softened slightly. Transfer to a clean glass jar, cover with the lid and refrigerate until cold. Chill for at least 3 hours and up to 5 days.

For the turkey, preheat the oven to 180°C/350°F/Gas Mark 4 and line a rimmed baking sheet with baking parchment. Set aside.

Mix the salt, sage, rosemary, thyme and pepper together in a bowl. Brush the olive oil over the turkey, then rub the turkey with the seasoning blend until coated all over.

Put the turkey on the prepared baking sheet and cook until a meat thermometer registers 74°C/165°F in the centre of the thickest part of the meat. Check the temperature after 45 minutes, then every 10–15 minutes until it is cooked through and at the correct temperature.

To make the sandwiches, slice the rolls and spread the bottom halves with mustard. Top with sliced turkey, relish and the tops of the roll.

SPINACH PASTA WITH FETA & PEAS

If you prefer a dairy-free dish, replace the feta with crumbled extra-firm tofu, which has been marinated overnight in lemon juice and very finely chopped garlic, then drained and sprinkled with salt.

Serves 4

1 quantity fresh homemade spinach pasta, cut into fettuccine (*see* page 78)

salt and freshly ground black pepper

200 g/7 oz/1½ cup peas, frozen or fresh

2 tbsp olive oil

2 tbsp white wine vinegar

1 garlic clove, peeled and smashed

225 g/8 oz/⅔ cup feta cheese, crumbled

1 handful dill, chopped

Fill a large saucepan with water, add ½ teaspoon salt and bring to the boil. When boiling, add the pasta and cook for 4–5 minutes or until *al dente*, adding the peas to the boiling water in the last 1 minute. Drain and rinse under cold running water briefly to cool.

Meanwhile, whisk the oil, vinegar, ¼ teaspoon salt, ¼ teaspoon black pepper and the smashed garlic together.

When the pasta and peas are cooked, remove the garlic from the dressing and discard, then pour the dressing over the drained pasta. Add half of the feta and all the dill and toss together.

Top with the remaining feta and season to taste, if needed.

CHICKEN MANGO CURRY

This is one of my favourite dishes. If I don't have any salad, I will often add a chopped red (bell) pepper and 275 g/10 oz/2 cups green beans to add some vegetables to the dish.

Serves 4

3 tbsp olive or coconut oil

450 g/1 lb skinless, boneless chicken breasts or thighs, cut into 2.5 cm/1 inch pieces

2 small sweet onions, peeled and chopped

1 yellow or green (bell) pepper, chopped

4 garlic cloves, peeled and very finely chopped

2 tbsp very finely chopped ginger

2 tbsp gluten-free curry powder

2 ripe mangoes, peeled, stoned and diced

1½ tbsp cider vinegar

250 ml/8 fl oz/1 cup gluten-free chicken stock

40 g/1½ oz/¼ cup sultanas (golden raisins)

150 ml/5 fl oz/⅔ cup whole canned coconut milk

salt and freshly ground black pepper

To garnish and serve

20 g/¾ oz/⅓ cup very finely chopped coriander (cilantro) or spring onions (scallions)

60 g/2¼ oz/½ cup roasted salted cashews

cooked rice or quinoa

salad of choice

Heat 2 tablespoons of the oil in a large frying pan. Add half of the chicken and brown. Transfer the chicken to a bowl and brown the second batch of chicken, then add to the bowl.

Add the onions to the pan and cook, stirring occasionally, for 15 minutes until they begin to caramelize. Add the (bell) pepper(s) and remaining oil and cook for 7 minutes until the peppers begin to soften. Add the garlic, ginger and curry powder and cook, stirring constantly, for 1 minute.

Add the chicken, half of the diced mangoes, the vinegar and stock to the pan (add green beans here, if liked). Increase the heat and simmer, stirring occasionally, for 20–25 minutes until the chicken is cooked through and the liquid has reduced by half.

Add the remaining mango, sultanas (golden raisins), coconut milk and salt and pepper. Check the seasoning and adjust if necessary, then reduce the heat and simmer gently for 5–10 minutes until the curry sauce is the thickness you desire and the added mango has warmed through. Garnish the curry with coriander (cilantro) and cashews and serve with rice or quinoa and a salad.

SALMON WITH ASPARAGUS-DILL TOPPING

Cooking on a cedar plank is an easy way to add smoked flavour on your charcoal or gas barbecue grill. The flavour from the plank transfers best when it's barbecued over direct heat, but you can cook salmon on a cedar plank in the oven at a lower temperature. If cedar planks for cooking are not available in your local store, you can order them online.

Serves 4

For the salmon

- 1 cedar plank soaked in water
- 1 tbsp paprika
- ½ tbsp chili powder
- salt
- ¾ tsp each ground coriander, garlic powder, granulated sugar, mild curry powder, freshly ground black pepper
- 1 tsp dried thyme
- 1 large skinless salmon fillet, cut into 4 fillets, about 175 g/6 oz each

For the asparagus-dill topping

- 130 g/4½ oz/1 cup asparagus, steamed and very finely chopped
- 1 large shallot, peeled and chopped
- 2 spring onions (scallions), thinly sliced
- 2 tbsp olive oil
- 1 tbsp very finely chopped dill
- 2 garlic cloves, peeled and very finely chopped
- salt
- 1 lemon, cut in half

For the salmon, presoak the cedar plank in water for 1–4 hours before using. Place a bowl or plate on top to submerge the plank in the water.

When ready to cook the salmon, mix the paprika, chili powder, 1 teaspoon salt, the coriander, garlic powder, sugar, curry powder, pepper and thyme together.

Preheat the barbecue to 200°C/400°F. Season the cedar plank with a little salt and place on the grill for 3–5 minutes, until it starts to smoke and crackle.

Place the salmon, skin-side down, on the plank and rub with the spice mixture.

For the topping, mix the asparagus, shallots, spring onions (scallions), olive oil, dill and garlic together in a bowl. Season with salt and the juice of half of the lemon and mix again.

Barbecue the fish on the cedar plank for 10–15 minutes over direct heat, or for 15–20 minutes over indirect heat. Keep a water spray bottle next to the grill to spritz the edges of the cedar plank if they catch alight. It's normal for the plank to char or even catch alight a little. Alternatively, place the plank in an oven preheated to 160°C/325°F/Gas Mark 3 and bake for 25 minutes.

Spoon the topping onto the fish and cook for a further 5–10 minutes until the fish is cooked through and flakes easily. Cut the reserved lemon half into wedges and serve with the salmon.

STIR-FRY SOBA NOODLES

This is a healthy, vibrant soba noodle recipe full of fresh vegetables and tender chicken. As the seasons change, replace the vegetables with those that reflect the season; asparagus in the spring, (bell) peppers in the summer, pak choi in the autumn and kale in the winter.

Serves 4

For the sauce

1½ tbsp gluten-free white miso paste (optional)

100 ml/3½ fl oz/⅓ cup gluten-free soy sauce

50 ml/2 fl oz/¼ cup gluten-free chicken stock

1 tbsp toasted sesame oil

1 tbsp honey

¼ tsp crushed dried chili (pepper) flakes

¼ tsp ground white pepper

For the chicken

450 g/1 lb boneless, skinless chicken breasts, thinly sliced, or chicken strips (tenders), thinly sliced

1–2 tbsp vegetable oil

For the soba and vegetables

175 g/6 oz gluten-free certified soba noodles

1 tbsp groundnut (peanut) or vegetable oil

200 g/7 oz/1½ cups green beans

1 medium carrot, peeled and cut into strips

1 hot chili (pepper), deseeded and thinly sliced

To serve

3 spring onions (scallions)

4 tbsp sesame seeds

1 lime, cut into wedges

For the sauce, whisk all the ingredients together and set aside.

For the chicken, mix 50 ml/2 fl oz/¼ cup of the sauce with the chicken and set aside.

For the soba noodles and vegetables, bring a large saucepan of water to the boil. Once boiling, add the noodles and cook for 5 minutes before draining and rinsing with cold water. Set aside.

Heat half the oil in a wok or frying pan. Working in two batches, stir-fry the chicken until browned and cooked through. Transfer to a bowl and set aside.

Add the remaining oil to the wok, plus extra if needed, and stir-fry the vegetables until crisp and tender. Add the chicken to the wok with the noodles, then pour in the remaining sauce and stir-fry until the sauce is absorbed and everything is heated through.

Serve with onions and sesame seeds and offer lime wedges to squeeze over before eating.

CANNELLINI BEAN STEW

This hearty stew makes a comforting meal on cold winter evenings. It also freezes well.

Serves 4

1 tbsp olive oil

350 g/12 oz packet spicy sausages (turkey, chicken or pork), sliced

1 onion, peeled and chopped

275 g/10 oz/1⅔ cups cherry tomatoes

4 large garlic cloves, peeled and very finely chopped

550 g/1 lb 3 oz/3 cups cooked cannellini beans or canned, rinsed and well drained

500 ml/18 fl oz/2 cups gluten-free chicken stock

125 ml/4 fl oz/½ cup white wine or more gluten-free chicken stock

1 tbsp thyme leaves or very finely chopped rosemary

125 g/4 oz/2 cups chopped kale or spinach leaves

1 tbsp balsamic vinegar

salt and freshly ground black pepper

very finely chopped parsley, to garnish

Heat the oil in a large saucepan and fry the sausage until browned and cooked through.

Add the onion and fry for 5–7 minutes until translucent, then add the tomatoes and garlic and fry for a further 2 minutes. Add the cannellini beans, stock, wine and thyme, then add the kale, if using. Increase the heat and simmer until the tomatoes have burst and the soup is hot. If you have added kale, simmer for 3–5 minutes until the kale is wilted and tender.

Stir in the vinegar and season to taste. If using spinach, stir in and cook for 1 minute until wilted. Sprinkle over the parsley and serve.

DINNER PARTY DISHES

ROAST CHICKEN

There are few dishes more delicious than a perfectly roasted chicken. Wonderful to serve for guests or as a weekend meal with the family, you can use different seasonings to flavour the chicken any way you like!

Serves 8

1 tbsp olive oil

1 large onion, cut into thick slices

1 (2.3–2.6 kg/5–6 lb) roasting chicken, giblets, excess fat and leftover feathers removed

salt and freshly ground black pepper

1 large bunch thyme

1 lemon, halved

1 head garlic, cut in half crossways

25 g/1 oz/2 tbsp/¼ stick butter or coconut oil, melted

Preheat the oven to 220°C/425°F/Gas Mark 7. Brush the oil in the bottom of a roasting pan and lay the onion slices on top. Set aside.

Pat the outside of the chicken dry, liberally season the inside, then stuff the cavity with the thyme, lemon and garlic. Brush the outside with the butter and season.

Tie the legs together with kitchen string and tuck the wing tips under the chicken. Place the chicken on top of the onion and roast for 20 minutes. Lower the oven temperature to 180°C/350°F/Gas Mark 4 and roast for another hour, or until the juices run clear. Roasting time will be 20 minutes per 450 g/1 lb chicken, plus an additional 20 minutes.

Transfer the chicken to a platter and cover with foil for 10 minutes before serving.

BAKED POLENTA
with Tomatoes & Caramelized Onions

This is a great gluten-free option that everyone will enjoy. It can be used as a base for any toppings you fancy.

Serves 6-8

1 tbsp extra virgin olive oil, plus extra for oiling

250 g/9 oz/1½ cups finely ground polenta (cornmeal)

salt and freshly ground black pepper

500 ml/18 fl oz/2 cups cold water

50 g/2 oz/½ cup grated Parmesan cheese or dairy-free substitute

25 g/1 oz/¼ cup thinly sliced onion, cooked until caramelized

150 g/5 oz/1 cup cherry tomatoes, sliced

125 g/4 oz chilled goat's cheese, cut into cubes, or dairy-free cream cheese
   substitute mixed with 1 tsp lemon juice

15 g/½ oz/¼ cup loosely packed slivered flat-leaf parsley leaves

Preheat the oven to 190°C/375°F/Gas Mark 5. Oil a 25 cm/10 inch tart pan with a removable bottom. Set aside.

Combine the polenta (cornmeal), ¼ teaspoon salt, pepper to taste and water in a saucepan. Bring to the boil, then reduce the heat to a simmer, stirring for 5 minutes. Stir in the grated Parmesan and stir for a further 3–5 minutes until smooth. Scoop the polenta into the tart pan and spread evenly over the bottom. Scatter with the onions and bake for 30 minutes until dry and crisp at the edges. Sprinkle with the tomatoes and goat's cheese, then bake for a further 5–10 minutes until the cheese is softened.

Remove from the pan, garnish with parsley and drizzle with oil. Season to taste.

SALMON EN CROUTE

This is a classic French dish with salmon and asparagus tucked inside puff pastry and baked until golden brown.

Serves 6

450 g/1 lb thin asparagus spears

salt and freshly ground black pepper

50 g/2 oz/¼ cup crème fraîche or dairy-free sour cream substitute

3 tbsp chopped dill

very finely chopped zest of 1 lemon

6 salmon fillets, 175 g/6 oz each, skinned and bones removed

1 quantity cold Croissant dough (*see* page 97), thawed, if previously frozen

gluten-free flour, for dusting

1 egg, lightly beaten with 1 tbsp water

Preheat the oven to 230°C/450°F/Gas Mark 8.

Trim the tips from the asparagus. Reserve the stems. Poach the tips in a pan of boiling salted water for 3–5 minutes until tender, then plunge into iced water and drain well. Set aside.

Pulse the asparagus stems in a food processor until very finely chopped, then mix with the crème fraîche, dill and lemon zest in a bowl. Season and set aside.

Cut the dough in half. Roll out into a long rectangle on a lightly floured surface and cut into 3 sections. On each section, lay one salmon fillet, leaving enough room to wrap the dough over the top. Top each fillet with one sixth of the asparagus mixture and one sixth of the asparagus tips, then repeat with the remaining dough, salmon and asparagus.

Brush the edges of the pastry with egg wash. Fold the dough over the salmon and press the edges to seal. Make 2–3 slits in the top, brush with egg wash and bake for 20–25 minutes until puffed and golden brown. Cool for 5 minutes before slicing.

BAKED MEATBALLS & ROASTED VEGETABLE SAUCE

Serve these meatballs with toasted Gluten-free Baguettes (*see* page 114) spread with garlic butter.

Serves 6

For the sauce

2 tbsp olive oil

5 shallots, peeled and trimmed

125 g/4 oz/¾ cup cherry tomatoes, halved

2 red (bell) peppers, deseeded and cut into 4 cm/1½ inch pieces

salt and freshly ground black pepper

800 g/1¾ lb (28 oz) canned chopped tomatoes

2 tbsp tomato purée (paste)

4 garlic cloves, peeled and very finely chopped

½ tbsp thyme leaves

For the meatballs

700 g/1½ lb lean minced (ground) beef or turkey

1 medium (large) egg

50 g/2 oz/¼ cup fine plain, dry, gluten-free breadcrumbs, made from an air-dried slice of gluten-free bread, crushed

20 g/¾ oz/⅓ cup parsley, very finely chopped

1 garlic clove, peeled and very finely chopped

½ tsp each dried oregano, dried thyme, salt

¼ tsp ground black pepper, or to taste

For the sauce, preheat the oven to 200°C/400°F/Gas Mark 6. Toss the oil with the shallots, cherry tomatoes and (bell) peppers in a casserole dish. Season and roast for 15 minutes, then stir. Add the tomatoes, tomato purée (paste), garlic and thyme. Stir, then lower the oven temperature to 180°C/350°F/Gas Mark 4 and return the vegetables to the oven.

For the meatballs, line a baking sheet with baking parchment. Mix all the ingredients together. Using your hands, form the mixture into balls about the size of golf balls and place them on the baking sheet. Remove the sauce from the oven. Stir and set aside. Bake the meatballs for 20 minutes.

Stir the sauce and add the meatballs, spooning the sauce over them. Bake for a further 20 minutes until the meatballs are cooked through.

VEGETARIAN 'MEATBALLS'

Don't eat meat? No problem! Try these tasty morsels instead.

Serves 6

1 tbsp olive oil

60 g/2¼ oz/½ cup very finely chopped white onion

3 garlic cloves, peeled and very finely chopped

225 g/8 oz gluten-free tempeh or 250 g/9 oz/1½ heaping cups canned chickpeas, rinsed and drained

75 g/3 oz/scant 1 cup dry gluten-free breadcrumbs or dairy-free substitute

65 g/2½ oz/scant 1 cup vegetarian Italian hard cheese or dairy-free substitute

1 medium (large) egg or 1 tbsp ground flaxseed mixed with 3 tbsp hot water and set aside for 5 minutes

3 tbsp very finely chopped parsley

2 tbsp marinara, tomato sauce or sauce from Baked Meatballs &
    Roasted Vegetable Sauce (*see* page 182)

2 tsp Italian seasoning

salt and freshly ground black pepper

olive oil, for cooking

Preheat the oven to 190°C/375°F/Gas Mark 5.

Heat the oil in a frying pan and fry the onion and garlic for 5–7 minutes until the onion is translucent. Set aside.

Pulse the tempeh, onion, garlic, 50 g/2 oz/½ cup of the breadcrumbs, 33 g/1¼ oz/⅓ cup of the Parmesan, the egg, parsley, sauce, Italian seasoning and salt and pepper together in a food processor. Do not purée; leave texture. Using your hands, form the mixture into balls the size of a golf ball. Mix the remaining breadcrumbs and Parmesan together on a plate, then roll the balls in the mixture to coat.

Heat the oil in a frying pan. Working in 2 batches, fry the balls for 5 minutes until browned, then add the balls to the sauce and continue to cook as in the Meatballs & Roasted Vegetable Sauce recipe.

Note

If you would like to use these in another recipe, bake them in an oven preheated to 180°C/350°F/Gas Mark 4 for a further 15 minutes before using.

GARLIC & ROSEMARY ROAST LAMB

To really taste the garlic and rosemary throughout the roast, stud the lamb a day in advance, cover and chill.

Serves 6-8

For the roast lamb

1 leg of lamb, bone in (about 2.7–3.4 kg/6–7½ lb)

8 garlic cloves, 4 peeled and thinly sliced and 4 peeled and very finely chopped

50 ml/2 fl oz/¼ cup fresh lemon juice 3 tbsp very finely chopped rosemary leaves

1 tbsp salt

2 tsp coarsely ground black pepper

For the sauce

20 g/¾ oz/⅓ cup chopped rosemary

20 g/¾ oz/⅓ cup chopped chives

20 g/¾ oz/⅓ cup chopped parsley

325 g/11½ oz/2 cups diced onions

500 ml/18 fl oz/2 cups chicken stock

250 ml/8 fl oz/1 cup red wine

Using a sharp knife, make several small incisions all over the meat, then push a garlic slice into each incision. Place the lamb in a metal roasting pan.

Mix the lemon juice, very finely chopped garlic and rosemary together. Brush over the lamb and season. If you are letting the mixture sit on the lamb to marinate it, cover and refrigerate for at least 2 hours. Let the lamb come to room temperature 1 hour before roasting.

Preheat the oven to 200°C/400°F/Gas Mark 6 and roast the lamb for 30 minutes. Lower the oven temperature to 180°C/350°F/Gas Mark 4 and cook for 1 hour longer for medium-rare, or until a meat thermometer inserted into the centre registers 63–66°C/145–150°F. Remove the lamb from the pan, place on a platter, tent with foil and rest for 10–15 minutes before carving.

Make the sauce while the lamb is resting. Place the roasting pan on the hob (stove), add the herbs and onions and stir to combine with the meat juices. Add the stock and wine to deglaze the pan, scraping the bottom with a wooden spoon to release any bits of meat. Increase the heat to high and reduce the liquid until it is a sauce consistency. Strain before serving, if liked. Slice the lamb and serve with the sauce drizzled over the top.

SAUCES & STUFFINGS

BÉCHAMEL SAUCE

Béchamel is a classic white sauce that can be the base for so many things or add your favourite cheese to make a homemade cheese sauce for gluten-free mac 'n' cheese, nachos or to pour over vegetables.

Makes about 900 ml/ 30 fl oz/ 2¾ cups sauce

About 600 ml/1 pint/2½ cups milk or unsweetened dairy-free alternative

40 g/1½ oz/3 tbsp butter or coconut oil

5 tbsp sweet rice flour

salt and ground white pepper

dash freshly grated nutmeg (optional)

Warm the milk gently.

Melt the butter in a small pan. Sprinkle the flour over the melted butter and whisk for 3–5 minutes until the roux begins to dry slightly and just starts to become golden.

Add a quarter of the milk, drizzling in a little at a time while stirring, then whisk to remove lumps. Whisk in the remaining milk, mixing well. Whisk as the sauce thickens. It will be ready when your whisk leaves 'tracks' in the sauce. Taste and season with salt, pepper and nutmeg, if using. If it's too thick, thin it with up to 125 ml/4 fl oz/½ cup milk.

Cheese sauce: Turn the heat to low and add 125 g/4 oz/1 cup grated cheese a little at a time, whisking until melted. Whisk in a dash of dry mustard and paprika. Add a little hot sauce to taste, if liked.

GRAVY

A flavourful gravy is a great accompaniment to any roast, whether it is turkey, chicken, lamb or beef.

Makes 1 litre/ 1³/₄ pints/ 4 cups

250–500 ml/8–18 fl oz/1–2 cups pan juices from a roast chicken, turkey, etc.

750 ml/1¼ pints/3 cups gluten-free beef, chicken or turkey stock

4 tbsp cornflour (cornstarch)

½ tsp garlic and/or onion powder

½ tsp paprika

½ tsp sage, thyme or rosemary (optional)

1–2 tbsp gluten-free Worcestershire sauce (optional)

salt and freshly ground black pepper

Remove the roast meat from the roasting pan and skim off excess fat, leaving about 1 tablespoon. Place the pan on top of the hob (stove), add 250 ml/8 fl oz/1 cup of the stock and bring to the boil while scraping up the browned bits.

Whisk the cornflour (cornstarch) into a cup of the remaining cold stock, then whisk the mixture into the pan and whisk while it cooks. Add the remaining stock, whisking until smooth and thickened. Add more stock if needed to thin and a little cornflour mixed in a small amount of cold water to thicken.

Whisk in the garlic powder, paprika and sage, thyme or rosemary, if using. Add the Worcestershire sauce if making beef gravy. Season.

STUFFING

I put a lot of roasted garlic in my stuffing, as roasting mellows and caramelizes its flavour. To roast the garlic, remove the top quarter of the bulbs, drizzle with olive oil, and bake until soft in an oven preheated to 200°C/400°F/Gas Mark 6 for 30–35 minutes.

Serves 10–12

For stuffing bread

1 tsp each garlic powder and dried onion powder

1½ tsp each dried basil, dried ground sage, celery seeds, dried parsley

1 quantity Basic Gluten-free Bread ingredients (*see* page 74)

For the stuffing

9 tbsp butter or olive oil, plus extra for greasing

95 g/3¼ oz/¾ cup carrots, peeled and cut into 5 mm/¼ inch dice

325 g/11½ oz/2 cups onion, peeled and cut into 5 mm/¼ inch dice

150 g/5 oz/1½ cups celery, cut into 5 mm/¼ inch dice

1.6 kg/3½ lb/8 cups stuffing bread, cut into ½–¾ inch cubes

700 g/1½ lb gluten-free sausage of choice (sweet or spicy), casing removed

2 tbsp poultry seasoning

2 tbsp finely chopped sage

salt and freshly ground black pepper

750 ml–1 litre/1¼–1¾ pints/3–4 cups gluten-free chicken stock

3 bulbs roasted garlic (see intro)

200 g/7 oz/1½ cups crisp apple, diced

100 g/3½ oz/1 cup chestnuts, walnuts, or pecans (optional)

For the stuffing bread, add the herbs and spices to the dry ingredients of the Basic Gluten-free Bread and follow the instructions for making the bread.

Preheat the oven to 190°C/375°F/Gas Mark 5. Grease a 23 x 33 cm/9 x 13 inch baking dish and set aside.

Heat 5 tablespoons of the butter or oil in a large frying pan and fry the carrots for 2 minutes until they begin to soften. Add the onion and celery and fry for 8–10 minutes until the onions are translucent. Combine the vegetables and stuffing bread cubes.

In the same pan, fry the sausage, stirring frequently with a wooden spoon to break up large pieces, for 8 minutes until browned and cooked. Remove the sausage with a slotted spoon and mix with the bread mixture, together with the poultry seasoning, sage, 1½ teaspoons salt and 2 teaspoons pepper. Discard any rendered fat from the pan. Add the stock, 250 ml/8 fl oz/1 cup at a time and mix. The stuffing should be well moistened.

Squeeze the garlic from their skins and mix gently into the bread mixture, keeping them whole. Add the apple and season. Transfer to the baking dish, drizzle the remaining butter or oil over the top of the stuffing and bake for 45–50 minutes until the top is golden.

MUSTARD

Mustard is one of the most varied of condiments, used in recipes ranging from grainy and sweet to searingly hot. Although it's harmless for most people, those on a gluten-free diet should still be wary. For example, the vinegars used in some mustards might not be gluten-free, and some additives and stabilizers can be derived from wheat. You can make your own to counter that problem, using a certified gluten-free brand of dry mustard.

As an alternative, you might opt to grind your own mustard seed. Purchase white, yellow, brown or black mustard seeds and experiment to see which you prefer. Commercial dry mustards often mix milder and more pungent varieties, so there's plenty of room for experimentation. It is best to buy your seeds in a sealed packet, from a guaranteed gluten-free source.

How hot your mustard will be will not only be determined by the type of mustard seed you use (yellow are the mildest with black being the hottest), but also will be determined by the temperature of the water used in the recipe. Use cold water for a hotter mustard and hot water for a mild mustard.

Finally, let your mustard set in the refrigerator or a cool place for at least a day before serving. Bitterness is a natural result of the mustard reaction, but will fade after a day or so.

Makes about 250 ml/ 8 fl oz/ 1 cup

6 tbsp mustard seeds (I used a mixture of yellow and brown, use only yellow if you prefer it milder)

50 g/2 oz/½ cup gluten-free mustard powder

100 ml/3½ fl oz/⅓ cup water (cold water for hot, spicy mustard, or hot water for mild mustard)

2 tsp salt

3 tbsp white wine vinegar, raspberry vinegar or cider vinegar

1 tbsp honey or granulated sugar

herbs, such as dill or rosemary (optional)

Using a mortar and pestle, grind the mustard seeds finely for a smooth mustard or coarsely for a grainy mustard. Add the mustard seeds to a small bowl together with the mustard powder and water and stir until well combined. Leave to stand for 15 minutes.

Stir in the salt, vinegar and honey and herbs, if using. If you want this really mild, gently heat the mixture in a saucepan for a few minutes. Place the mixture in a clean jam jar, cover and chill for at least 12 hours or overnight to allow the flavour to mellow. It will be too strong to use straight away. Store in the refrigerator for up to a month.

CAKES, TREATS & DESSERTS

CRANBERRY & OAT CRUMBLE PIE

Pears join cranberries in this sweet crumble. If pears aren't available, use apples instead.

Serves 8

For the topping

150 g/5 oz/1 cup Rice-sorghum Flour Blend, *see* page 73 (or combine 100 g/3½
   oz/⅔ cup white rice flour, 3 tbsp potato starch and 2 tbsp tapioca flour)

50 g/2 oz/¼ cup granulated sugar

½ tsp ground ginger

¼ tsp salt

125 g/4 oz/½ cup/1 stick cold unsalted butter or coconut oil, cut into cubes

95 g/3¼ oz/1 cup gluten-free certified old-fashioned rolled oats

50 g/2 oz/½ cup chopped toasted pecans or walnuts (optional)

For the filling

vegetable oil, for oiling

400 g/14 oz/4 cups fresh or frozen cranberries

2 pears, peeled and chopped

2 tsp very finely chopped orange zest

1 tbsp fresh orange juice

2 tbsp cornflour (cornstarch)

100 g/3½ oz/½ cup sugar, plus up to 3 tbsp extra if needed, depending on how tart
   the fruit is

Pulse the flour blend, the 50 g/2 oz/¼ cup sugar, the ginger and salt in a food processor until combined. Add the butter and pulse just until the mixture forms large clumps with none larger than the size of a pea. Transfer the mixture to a bowl and toss with the oats and nuts, if using. Cover and chill until ready to use.

Preheat the oven to 180°C/350°F/Gas Mark 4. Oil a 25 cm/10 inch round baking dish or two 13 cm/5 inch round baking dishes and line a baking sheet with foil.

For the filling, toss the cranberries, pears, orange zest and juice together in another bowl. And in another bowl, stir the cornflour (cornstarch) and the 100 g/3½ oz/½ cup sugar together, then sprinkle the sugar mixture over the fruit and toss to combine. Transfer the cranberry mixture to the baking dish(es) and top with the cold oat mixture.

Place the crumble on the baking sheet and bake until bubbling and the top is golden brown, 45–50 minutes for the large dish or 30–35 minutes for the smaller dishes.

VEGAN CHOCOLATE ALMOND COOKIES

There's no need for butter or eggs to create a delicious chocolate cookie. Want even more decadence? Add up to 125 g/4 oz/¾ cup plain (semisweet) chocolate chips to the batter before baking.

Makes 24

185 g/6½ oz/1¼ cups Rice-sorghum Flour Blend (*see* page 73)

50 g/2 oz/½ cup cocoa powder

1 tsp cream of tartar

½ tsp xanthan gum

½ tsp bicarbonate of soda (baking soda)

¼ tsp salt

100 ml/3½ fl oz/⅓ cup neutral-tasting cooking oil

130 g/4½ oz/⅔ cup granulated sugar

125 ml/4 fl oz/½ cup unsweetened almond milk

½ tsp gluten-free vanilla extract

½ tsp gluten-free almond extract

½ cup chopped roasted salted almonds

Preheat the oven to 160°C/325°F/Gas Mark 3. Line 2 baking sheets with baking parchment.

Using a whisk, mix the rice flour blend, cocoa powder, cream of tartar, xanthan gum, bicarbonate of soda (baking soda) and salt together, being sure to work out any lumps of cocoa powder.

Combine the oil and sugar in a heavy-duty stand mixer fitted with the paddle attachment, mixing for 30 seconds on medium speed. Add the milk and vanilla and almond extracts and mix for a further 30 seconds, then scrape down the sides of bowl.

Add the dry ingredients to the wet ingredients and mix on low speed, scraping down the sides of the bowl as needed. Scoop out the dough in heaped tablespoonsful and place on the baking sheets, 12 per sheet. Using wet hands, roll the dough into balls. Sprinkle the tops with chopped almonds, pressing into the dough lightly so they stick.

Bake for 12 minutes, or until just set. Leave to cool for 5 minutes on the baking sheets before transferring to a wire rack to cool.

LEMON BARS

Lemon desserts were my grandfather's favourite treat. He would have loved these lemon bars with their bright lemony filling on a shortbread crust.

Makes 16

For the crust

50 ml/2 fl oz/¼ cup mild-flavoured
  oil, plus extra for oiling
100 g/3½ oz/⅔ cup finely
  ground rice flour
50 g/2 oz/¼ cup granulated sugar
50 g/2 oz/¼ cup potato starch (*not* flour)
1½ tbsp tapioca flour (starch)
1 tsp xanthan gum

For the filling

4 medium (large) eggs, room temperature
150 g/5 oz/¾ cup plus 2 tbsp sugar
125 ml/4 fl oz/½ cup lemon juice
1½ tbsp potato starch (*not* flour)
1 tbsp tapioca flour (starch)
2½ tsp very finely chopped lemon zest
½ tsp gluten-free baking powder
3 tbsp icing (confectioners') sugar

Preheat the oven to 180°C/350°F/Gas Mark 4. Line a 20 x 20 cm/8 x 8 inch cake pan with oiled foil or baking parchment, using two pieces the width of the pan, one going in each direction, allowing extra length to hang over the edges of the pan as handles.

Combine all the crust ingredients in a heavy-duty stand mixer. Beat on medium speed, scraping down the sides of the bowl frequently, until the mixture resembles coarse crumbs. Press onto the bottom of the baking pan and bake for 18–20 minutes until the edges are lightly browned.

Meanwhile, combine all the filling ingredients, except the icing (confectioners') sugar. Beat on low speed with the whisk attachment, scraping down the sides of the bowl frequently, until well mixed. Pour the filling over the partially baked crust and bake for 25–27 minutes until the filling is set. Cool in the pan on a wire rack.

Sprinkle with icing sugar while still warm and again when cool. After cooling to room temperature, chill the mixture. When ready to slice, use the foil or baking parchment handles to lift the mixture from the pan and set on a chopping (cutting) board. Carefully remove the foil from the sides and, using a large knife, cut into 16 bars.

MACARONS

Macarons always look like you put in so much more work to make them than you actually did! While not difficult to make, successful macarons are the result of following the technique to achieve the lovely shape.

Serves 16

130 g/4½ oz/1¼ cups plus 1 tsp icing (confectioners') sugar

125 g/4 oz/1 cup finely ground, blanched almonds

6 tbsp fresh egg whites, from about 3 large (extra large) eggs

scant ⅛ tsp salt

50 g/2 oz/¼ cup granulated sugar

For the macaron filling

3 medium (large) egg whites

200 g/7 oz/1 cup granulated sugar

225 g/8 oz/1 cup/2 sticks butter, room temperature, cut into pieces, or dairy-free alternative

Preheat the oven to 180°C/350°F/Gas Mark 4 and line two baking sheets with baking parchment. Whisk the icing (confectioners') sugar and ground almonds together in a medium bowl. Whisk the egg whites and salt together in a heavy-duty stand mixer fitted with the whisk attachment on medium speed until foamy. Increase the speed to high and gradually add the granulated sugar, continuing to whisk until stiff, glossy peaks form. Using a rubber spatula, fold in the almond mixture until incorporated.

Fit a piping (pastry) bag with an 8 mm/⅜ inch round nozzle (tip) and fill with the batter. Pipe 2.5 cm/1 inch discs onto the baking sheets, leaving 5 cm/2 inches between them to allow for expansion. Leave at room temperature for about 15 minutes until the batter looks dry, a soft skin forms on the tops of the macarons and the shiny surface turns dull.

Bake in the oven, with the oven door slightly ajar, for 15 minutes until the surface of the macarons is completely dry. Transfer the baking shees to a wire rack and leave the macarons to cool completely. Gently peel the macarons off the baking parchment. Be careful – their tops are fragile and can crack easily. Use immediately or store chilled in an airtight container for up to 2 days or frozen for up to 1 month.

For the filling, place the egg whites and sugar in a heavy-duty stand-mixer bowl. Set the bowl over a saucepan of simmering water and heat, whisking for 3–5 minutes until it feels warm to the touch and the sugar is dissolved. Transfer the bowl to the stand mixer. Using the whisk attachment, whisk the egg mixture on high speed for 3–5 minutes until it is stiff and shiny. Add the butter, a piece at a time, and continue to mix until the butter is thoroughly incorporated. Use immediately or keep, covered, for up to 1 week in the refrigerator. Bring to room temperature before stirring and filling the macarons.

To fill the macarons, fill a piping bag with the filling and turn the macarons so their flat bottoms face up. On half of them, pipe about 1 teaspoon of filling. Sandwich these with the remaining macarons, flat-side down, pressing slightly to spread the filling to the edges. Refrigerate for 1 hour until firm.

Variations

Coffee: Add 2–4 drops brown food colouring to the whisked egg whites. Combine the macaron filling with 2 tablespoons espresso powder dissolved in 1 tablespoon warm water.

Raspberry: Add 2–4 drops rose food colouring to the egg whites after they are whisked. Use seedless raspberry jam for the filling.

Cassis (blackcurrant): Add 2–4 drops purple food colouring to the egg whites after they are whisked. Use blackcurrant jam for the filling.

Pistachio: Add 2–4 drops green food colouring to the egg whites after they are whisked. Combine the macaron filling with 75 g/3 oz/¼ cup pistachio paste.

BROWNIES

These are my family's favourite brownies. Packed with chocolate, I hope you like them as much as we do!

Makes 12–16

6 tbsp mild-flavoured oil, plus extra for oiling

175 g/6 oz good-quality dark gluten-free (and dairy-free if preferred) dark (semisweet) chocolate, chopped

225 g/8 oz/1 cup packed soft brown sugar

40 g/1½ oz/⅓ cup Bean Flour Blend (see page 70)

30 g/1¼ oz/⅓ cup cocoa powder

¼ tsp gluten-free baking powder

3 medium (large) eggs, beaten

Oil a 25 x 18 cm/10 x 7 inch or 23 x 23 cm/9 x 9 inch cake pan with baking parchment. Lightly oil the paper.

Melt the chocolate, oil and sugar in a saucepan, stirring so the ingredients are properly combined. Transfer to a bowl and leave to cool slightly. Sift the flour, cocoa powder and baking powder into the mixture and stir well. Add the beaten eggs and stir until well blended.

Pour the batter into the pan and leave to stand for 30 minutes.

Preheat the oven to 180°C/350°F/Gas Mark 4.

Bake for about 35 minutes. Test by inserting a cocktail stick (toothpick) into the centre to check that it's cooked through. Leave to cool completely in the pan, then cut into bars.

LEMON SOUFFLÉ
with Raspberry Sauce

There is something magical that happens when a soufflé is baked, transforming the frothy batter into a delicate, lofty pastry.

Serves 6

For the raspberry sauce

150 g/5 oz/1¼ cups raspberries, or 350 g/12 oz/scant 3 cups frozen, thawed

3 tbsp granulated sugar, or to taste

2 tbsp freshly squeezed lemon juice, or to taste

For the soufflé

15 g/½ oz/1 tbsp butter, melted, or coconut oil, plus extra for coating the ramekins

50 g/2 oz/¼ cup granulated sugar, plus extra for the ramekins

4 medium (large) egg yolks, plus 5 large egg whites, room temperature

1 tbsp Rice-sorghum Flour Blend (*see* page 73) or sweet rice flour

1 tbsp very finely chopped lemon zest; ¼ tsp salt

125 ml/4 fl oz/½ cup whole milk or unsweetened dairy-free alternative, such as almond

3 tbsp freshly squeezed lemon juice; icing (confectioners') sugar, to decorate (optional)

For the sauce, purée all the ingredients in a blender or food processor until smooth. Strain through a sieve (strainer) into a plastic container. Cover and chill until ready to serve.

For the soufflés, brush the bottom and sides of six 175 g/6 oz ramekins with melted butter. Sprinkle a little sugar into each ramekin and tilt the ramekin so that the sugar lightly coats the sides. Tip any excess out.

Whisk the yolks, flour, lemon zest, 1 tablespoon of the sugar and salt together until smooth.

Heat the milk until just steaming. While whisking constantly, very slowly add 2 tablespoons of the hot milk to the egg yolk mixture, then slowly drizzle the egg yolk mixture into the remaining hot milk in the pan, still whisking. Cook over a medium heat, whisking until it has thickened to a loose pudding texture. Strain the mixture through a sieve into a large bowl. Whisk in the melted butter and lemon juice. Smooth plastic wrap over the surface and chill for 30 minutes.

Preheat the oven to 190°C/375°F/Gas Mark 5. Beat the egg whites until frothy, then, while whisking, gradually add the remaining 3 tablespoons sugar. Whisk until stiff peaks form. Fold one quarter of the whites at a time into the lemon mixture, then divide the batter between the ramekins. Gently smooth the tops and set the ramekins in a roasting pan. Place in the oven and carefully pour boiling water into the bottom of the pan. Bake for 14–17 minutes until puffed and light golden brown. Do not open the oven while the soufflés are baking. Dust with icing (confectioners') sugar, if liked, and serve with the sauce.

HOMEMADE ICE-CREAM CONES

If I have time, it is nice to pour a little melted chocolate into the bottom of a chilled cone. This prevents any leaks and makes the last bite an extra special treat. Be sure to allow the batter to chill and 'rest' for a more sturdy final product.

Makes 8

150 g/5 oz/1 cup Rice-sorghum Flour Blend (*see* page 73)

⅔ tsp xanthan gum

¼ tsp salt

2 medium (large) eggs

100 g/3½ oz/½ cup granulated sugar

50 ml/2 fl oz/¼ cup milk or dairy-free substitute

50 g/2 oz/4 tbsp/¼ cup/½ stick butter or non-hydrogenated shortening, melted

1 tsp gluten-free vanilla extract

Mix the flour blend, xanthan gum and salt together and set aside.

Whisk the eggs and sugar together in a large bowl until thickened. Mix in the dry ingredients, the milk, melted butter and vanilla until incorporated. Cover with plastic wrap and chill for several hours at least, or overnight.

To make the cones, follow the instructions on an ice-cream cone iron using 2 tablespoons batter per cone.

SPICED PUMPKIN & RUM ROLL

If you haven't made a cake roll before, give this one a try! Pumpkin gives a lot of moisture and flexibility to the cake, making this simple to assemble, yet the presentation will impress your family.

Serves 8

For the spiced pumpkin cake

vegetable oil or butter, for greasing

100 g/3½ oz/¾ cup Bean Flour Blend (*see* page 70)

1 tsp gluten-free baking powder

1 tsp ground cinnamon

¾ tsp ground ginger

½ tsp each salt, xanthan gum

¼ tsp ground nutmeg

3 medium (large) eggs

200 g/7 oz/1 cup granulated sugar

165 g/5¾ oz/⅔ cup canned pumpkin

icing (confectioners') sugar, for sprinkling

For the rum cream filling

225 g/8 oz/1 cup cream cheese, at room temperature, or dairy-free alternative

100 g/3½ oz/1 cup icing (confectioners') sugar

1 tbsp rum, plus extra if needed or milk, if preferred

1 tsp gluten-free vanilla extract

Preheat the oven to 190°C/375°F/Gas Mark 5. Line a 38 x 25 cm/15 x 10 inch Swiss roll (jelly roll) pan with baking parchment. Lightly grease the baking parchment and set aside.

Combine the flour blend, baking powder, cinnamon, ginger, salt, xanthan gum and nutmeg and set aside.

Place the eggs and sugar in a heavy-duty stand mixer fitted with the whisk attachment and beat until thick and creamy. Add the pumpkin and mix until combined. Add the flour mixture and mix until just combined. Spread the cake batter onto the baking parchment and bake for 13–15 minutes until the cake springs back when touched.

Place a clean tea (dish) towel on a work surface and sprinkle generously with icing (confectioners') sugar. Carefully flip the warm cake onto the towel and gently peel back the parchment. Roll up the cake and towel together, then cool completely.

For the filling, using a freestanding electric or hand mixer fitted with the whisk attachment, beat all the ingredients together until creamy. Add more rum if the filling is too thick. Carefully unroll the cooled cake and spread on the filling in an even layer. Roll the cake back up, removing the towel. Wrap the cake in plastic wrap and chill for several hours to firm up. When ready to serve, unwrap, dust with icing sugar and cut into slices.

PASSION FRUIT ICE-CREAM CAKE

An ice-cream cake is not a lot of work, but it does take some time. Start a couple of days ahead of when you want it to allow time for each layer to freeze. See the photo on page 4.

Serves 16

For the chestnut cake

130 g/4½ oz/1⅓ cups finely ground chestnut flour

1½ tsp gluten-free baking powder

75 g/3 oz/½ cup plus 2 tbsp brown sugar

100 g/3½ oz/6½ tbsp salted butter, at room temperature, or dairy-free alternative

3 medium (large) eggs

2 tbsp milk or dairy-free milk substitute, plus 1 extra tbsp, if needed

For the ice-cream cake

2 litres/3½ pints/8½ cups vanilla ice cream or dairy-free substitute, such as one made from coconut milk

1 frozen chestnut cake in springform pan

1 quantity passion fruit filling

1 quantity passion fruit topping

For the passion fruit filling

150 g/5 oz/¾ cup granulated sugar

25 g/1 oz/¼ cup cornflour (cornstarch)

250 ml/8 fl oz/1 cup passion fruit nectar or purée

4 medium (large) egg yolks

1 vanilla pod (bean), split in half lengthways, seeds reserved

8 tbsp unsalted butter, cut into tablespoons, or dairy-free alternative

For the passion fruit topping

4 whole passionfruit

100 g/3½ oz/½ cup caster (superfine) sugar

7.5 cm/3 inch strip orange zest

2 tbsp water

For the chestnut cake, preheat the oven to 160°C/325°F/Gas Mark 3. Line the bottom of a 23 cm/9 inch springform cake pan with baking parchment and set aside. Sift the chestnut flour with the baking powder into a bowl. Add the remaining ingredients, then, using a hand mixer, whisk together until the mixture is well incorporated.

Pour the cake batter into the pan and bake for 18–20 minutes until a cocktail stick (toothpick) inserted into the centre comes out clean. Leave to cool in the pan, then remove and peel off the baking parchment. Place the cake back in the pan, cover with plastic wrap and freeze until ready to assemble.

For the filling, whisk the sugar and cornflour (cornstarch) together in a double boiler or in a heatproof bowl set over a pan of simmering water. Whisk in the passion fruit nectar, egg yolks and vanilla seeds until very smooth. Cook over a medium heat, whisking constantly, until thick. Remove from the heat and whisk in the butter, 1 tablespoon at a time, until incorporated. Scrape the filling into a bowl. Press a sheet of plastic wrap on the surface and chill for about 2 hours.

For the topping, scoop out the flesh and seeds of the passion fruit. Put into a food processor with the caster (superfine) sugar and pulse for 10–15 seconds. Pour into a sieve (strainer) over a bowl and rub with a spoon until only the seeds remain in the sieve. Add 1–2 teaspoons of the seeds back into the purée, if liked. Combine the pulp, zest and water in a saucepan. Cook, stirring, for 3–5 minutes until the sugar dissolves. Bring to the boil, then reduce the heat and simmer, uncovered, for 5–6 minutes until the syrup thickens slightly. Remove and discard the zest. Chill in a covered container.

To assemble, whisk half of the ice cream in a heavy-duty stand mixer for 2 minutes until fluffy but still frozen. Remove the cake from the freezer. Spread the ice cream up the sides of the pan, creating a thick layer all around the pan, making sure to connect to the cake. Spread any extra ice cream over the cake. Working quickly, scoop the passion fruit filling into the centre, smoothing into an even layer. Freeze for at least 4 hours, or overnight. Spread the remaining ice cream, also whisked, smoothly on top of the passion fruit layer, ensuring it is even with the top of the pan. Cover the top with another sheet of baking parchment and freeze overnight, or until completely solid.

When ready to serve, remove the cake from the freezer. Peel away the top layer of parchment and gently loosen the pan, wiggling it until it slides smoothly off the cake. Place the cake on a serving platter, pour over the passion fruit topping and serve.

OAT & NUT MUFFINS

These muffins are so moist and tender, you'll want them for dessert! If you don't have hazelnuts then use pecans instead.

Makes 18

325 g/11½ oz/3½ cups gluten-free rolled oats
or 275 g/10 oz/3 cups oat flour

1 tbsp gluten-free baking powder

½ tsp salt

½ tsp xanthan gum

½ tsp ground cinnamon

¼ tsp grated nutmeg

250 ml/8 fl oz/1 cup milk
or unsweetened dairy-free substitute

185 g/6½ oz/¾ cup apple purée (sauce)

110 g/3¾ oz/½ cup soft brown sugar

2 medium (large) eggs

3 tbsp vegetable oil

2 tsp finely shredded orange zest

1 tsp gluten-free vanilla extract

90 g/3¼ oz/¾ cup chopped toasted hazelnuts

50 g/2 oz/½ cup rolled oats, for topping

Place 18 paper cases (liners) in two 12-hole muffin pans. Set aside.

To make the oat flour, if needed, working in batches, blitz the oats in a blender until they form a fine, flour-like consistency. Stir the oat flour, baking powder, salt, xanthan gum, cinnamon and nutmeg together in a large bowl.

Mix the milk, apple purée (sauce), brown sugar, eggs, oil, orange zest and vanilla together in another bowl. Combine the wet and dry ingredients and mix until just combined. Leave for 10 minutes before stirring in the toasted hazelnuts.

Preheat the oven to 180°C/350°F/Gas Mark 4.

Pour the batter into the lined muffin pans, filling each three-quarters full. Sprinkle the batter with rolled oats and bake for 15–18 minutes until a cocktail stick (toothpick) inserted into the centre of one comes out clean.

INDEX

Entries with upper-case initials indicate recipes.

A
almonds & almond flour 46
    Almond Crepes 92
    Amaranth & Quinoa
        Porridge 88
    Basic Gluten-free Bread 74
    Curried Millet & Amaranth
        Bread 104
    Flatbread with Sesame
        Seeds 112
    Lemon Soufflé with Raspberry
        Sauce 212
    Macarons 206
    Seeded Honey Bread 102
    Vegan Chocolate Almond
        Cookies 202
Almond Crepes 92
amaranth 40, 46
    Amaranth & Quinoa
        Porridge 88
    Curried Millet & Amaranth
        Bread 104
    Margherita Pizza 120
Amaranth & Quinoa Porridge 88
Avocado & Lime Hummus 136

B
Baked Meatballs & Roasted
    Vegetable Sauce 182
Baked Polenta with Tomatoes &
    Caramelized Onions 178
Basic Gluten-free Bread 74
Bean Flour Blend 70
Béchamel Sauce 190
Beetroot Hummus 138
Brownies 210
buckwheat flour 45
    Buckwheat Gnocchi 146
    Pumpkin Seed Bread 100
Buckwheat Gnocchi 146

C
Cannellini Bean Stew 172
Carrot Loaf Cake with
    Cinnamon 106
Cauliflower Couscous 142
cheese
    Baked Polenta with Tomatoes
        & Caramelized Onions 179

Béchamel Sauce 190
Carrot Loaf Cake with
    Cinnamon 106
Garden Quiche 122
Margherita Pizza 120
Mini Quiches Lorraines 119
Mushroom, Leek & Cheese
    Tart 126
Spiced Pumpkin & Rum
    Roll 216
Spinach Pasta with Feta &
    Peas 163
Thai Chicken Pizza 128
Vegetarian 'Meatballs' 183
chicken 39
    Cannellini Bean Stew 173
    Chicken Mango Curry 166
    Chicken & Pomegranate
        Pilaf 141
    Garlic & Rosemary Roast
        Lamb 186
    Gravy 193
    Pumpkin Risotto 156
    Quinoa & Courgette Cakes 131
    Roast Chicken 176
    Roasted Pumpkin Soup 134
    Stir-fry Soba Noodles 170
    Stuffing 194
    Sweet & Sour Chicken 158
    Thai Chicken Pizza 128
Chicken & Pomegranate Pilaf 140
Chicken Mango Curry 166
Chickpea Courgette Waffles with
    Eggs 86
chickpeas & chickpea flour 45
    Avocado & Lime Hummus 136
    Basic Gluten-free Bread 74
    Beetroot Hummus 138
    Chickpea Courgette Waffles
        with Eggs 86
    Falafel 148
    Vegetarian 'Meatballs' 183
chocolate 18, 45
    Amaranth & Quinoa
        Porridge 88
    Brownies 211
    Homemade Ice-cream
        Cones 215
    Vegan Chocolate Almond
        Cookies 202
coeliac 6, 7, 15, 26, 28, 29, 31,
    32, 34, 35, 36, 56
cornflour (cornstarch) 48
    Basic Gluten-free Bread 74
    Bean Flour Blend 70
    Cranberry & Oat Crumble
        Pie 200

Gluten-free Croissants 96
Gravy 192
Homemade Pasta 78
Passion Fruit Ice-cream
    Cake 218
Rice-Sorghum Flour Blend 73
Shortcrust Pastry 76
Sweet & Sour Chicken 158
Corn Fritters 84
contamination 15, 16, 18, 22, 40,
    58, 61, 62, 64, 65, 67
Cranberry & Oat Crumble Pie 200
Curried Millet & Amaranth
    Bread 104

F
Falafel 148
Flatbread with Sesame Seeds 112
Flaxseed Rolls 110
foods that contain gluten 15
fruit 21, 40, 49, 55, 58
    Amaranth & Quinoa Porridge 88
    Avocado & Lime Hummus 136
    Cauliflower Couscous 142
    Chicken Mango Curry 166
    Cranberry & Oat Crumble
        Pie 200
    Golden Overnight Oats with
        Chia Pudding Variation 90
    Lemon Bars 204
    Lemon Soufflé with Raspberry
        Sauce 212
    Oat & Nut Muffins 220
    Passion Fruit Ice-cream
        Cake 218
    Rice-flour Pancakes 82
    Stuffing 194

G
Garden Quiche 122
Garlic & Rosemary Roast
    Lamb 186
Gluten-free Baguette 114
Gluten-free Croissants 96
going gluten free 52
Golden Overnight Oats with Chia
    Pudding Variation 90
Gravy 192

H
Homemade Ice-cream Cones 214
Homemade Pasta 78

K
key gluten-free foods 38

L
Lemon Bars 204

Lemon Soufflé with Raspberry
  Sauce 212

M
Macarons 206
Margherita Pizza 120
millet 40, 46
  Curried Millet & Amaranth
    Bread 104
  Pumpkin Seed Bread 100
Mini Quiches Lorraines 118
Mushroom, Leek & Cheese
  Tart 126
Mustard 196

N
nuts 39, 40, 46, 55
  Basic Gluten-free Bread 74
  Beetroot Hummus 138
  Carrot Loaf Cake with
    Cinnamon 106
  Chicken Mango Curry 166
  Cranberry & Oat Crumble
    Pie 200
  Oat & Nut Muffins 220
  Passion Fruit Ice-cream
    Cake 218
  Rice-Sorghum Flour Blend 73
  Stuffed Peppers with Quinoa &
    Walnuts 150
  Stuffing 194
  Thai Chicken Pizza 128

O
Oat & Nut Muffins 220
oats 15, 16, 29, 36, 40, 46
  Cranberry & Oat Crumble
    Pie 200
  Golden Overnight Oats with
    Chia Pudding Variation 90
  Lemon Soufflé 212
  Oat & Nut Muffins 220
  Rice-flour Pancakes 82

P
Passion Fruit Ice-cream Cake 218
potato flour 46
  Lemon Bars 204
  Rice-sorghum Flour Blend 73
potato starch 46
  Basic Gluten-free Bread 74
  Cranberry & Oat Crumble
    Pie 200
  Flatbread with Sesame
    Seeds 112
  Gluten-free Baguette 114
  Homemade Pasta 78
  Lemon Bars 204

Pumpkin Seed Bread 100
Rice-sorghum Flour Blend 73
Seeded Honey Bread 102
Shortcrust Pastry 76
preparation & techniques 68
Pumpkin Risotto 156
Pumpkin Seed Bread 100

Q
quinoa 40, 46
  Amaranth & Quinoa
    Porridge 88
  Chicken Mango Curry 166
  Pumpkin Seed Bread 100
  Quinoa & Courgette Cakes 131
  Rice-Flour Pancakes 82
  Rice-Sorghum Flour Blend 73
  Seeded Honey Bread 102
  Stuffed Peppers with Quinoa &
    Walnuts 150
Quinoa & Courgette Cakes 130

R
Raisin Whirls 108
rice 16, 18, 40, 45, 46, 55, 56
  Basic Gluten-free Bread 74
  Béchamel Sauce 190
  Chicken Mango Curry 166
  Chicken & Pomegranate
    Pilaf 141
  Cranberry & Oat Crumble
    Pie 200
  Curried Millet & Amaranth
    Bread 104
  Flatbread with Sesame
    Seeds 112
  Gluten-free Croissants 97
  Homemade Ice-cream
    Cones 215
  Homemade Pasta 78
  Lemon Bars 204
  Lemon Soufflé with Raspberry
    Sauce 212
  Margherita Pizza 120
  Pumpkin Risotto 156
  Pumpkin Seed Bread 100
  Rice-flour Pancakes 82
  Rice-sorghum Flour Blend 73
  Seeded Honey Bread 102
  Shortcrust Pastry 76
  Sweet & Sour Chicken 158
  Thai Chicken Pizza 128
  Vegan Chocolate Almond
    Cookies 202
Rice-flour Pancakes 82
Rice-sorghum Flour Blend 72
Roast Chicken 176

Roast Turkey Sandwich with
  Cucumber Relish 160
Roasted Pumpkin Soup 134

S
Salmon en Croute 180
Salmon with Asparagus-dill
  topping 168
Seeded Honey Bread 102
Shortcrust Pastry 76
sorghum 40, 45
  Basic Gluten-free Bread 74
  Bean Flour Blend 70
  Flatbread with Sesame
    Seeds 112
  Gluten-free Baguette 114
  Gluten-free Croissants 96
  Rice-sorghum Flour Blend 72
  Shortcrust Pastry 76
  Vegan Chocolate Almond
    Cookies 202
Spinach Pasta with Feta &
  Peas 162
Spiced Pumpkin & Rum Roll 216
Stir-fry Soba Noodles 170
Stuffed Peppers with Quinoa &
  Walnuts 150
Stuffing 194
substitute 18, 46, 48
Sweet & Sour Chicken 158

T
tapioca flour (starch) 48
  Almond Crepes 92
  Basic Gluten-free Bread 74
  Bean Flour Blend 70
  Curried Millet & Amaranth
    Bread 104
  Flatbread with Sesame
    Seeds 112
  Gluten-free Baguette 114
  Lemon Bars 204
  Margherita Pizza 120
  Pumpkin Seed Bread 100
  Shortcrust Pastry 76
Thai Chicken Pizza 128
tools & equipment 60

V
Vegan Chocolate Almond
  Cookies 202
Vegetarian 'Meatballs' 183
Veggie Frittata with Dill 153

W
what is gluten? 12
whole grains 40
why gluten free? 26

If you enjoyed this book please sign up for updates,
information and offers on further titles in this series at
www.flametreepublishing.com